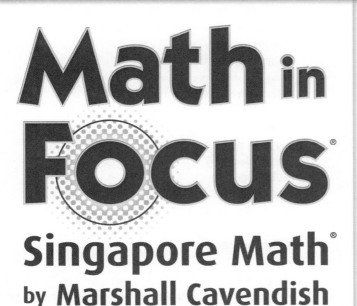

Reteach

Consultant and Author
Dr. Fong Ho Kheong

Author
Ang Kok Cheng

Marshall Cavendish
Education

U.S. Distributor

**Houghton
Mifflin
Harcourt**

© 2015 Marshall Cavendish Education Pte Ltd

Published by Marshall Cavendish Education
An imprint of Marshall Cavendish Education Pte Ltd
Times Centre, 1 New Industrial Road, Singapore 536196
Customer Service Hotline: (65) 6213 9444
US Office Tel: (1-914) 332 8888 Fax: (1-914) 332 8882
E-mail: tmesales@mceducation.com
Website: www.mceducation.com

Distributed by
Houghton Mifflin Harcourt
222 Berkeley Street
Boston, MA 02116
Tel: 617-351-5000
Website: www.hmheducation.com/mathinfocus

First published 2015

All rights reserved. Permission is hereby granted to teachers to reprint or photocopy in classroom quantities, for use by one teacher and his or her students only, the pages in this work that carry the appropriate copyright notice, provided each copy made shows the copyright notice. Such copies may not be sold, and further distribution is expressly prohibited. Except as authorized above, no part of this publication may be reproduced, stored in a retrieval system or transmitted, in any form or by any means, electronic, mechanical, photocopying, recording or otherwise, without the prior written permission of Marshall Cavendish Education.

Marshall Cavendish and *Math in Focus*® are registered trademarks of Times Publishing Limited.

Singapore Math® is a trademark of Singapore Math Inc® and Marshall Cavendish Education Pte Ltd.

Math in Focus® Reteach 1B
ISBN 978-0-544-19248-5

Printed in Singapore

2 3 4 5 6 7 8   1401   20 19 18 17 16 15
4500495934   A B C D E

Contents

Addition and Subtraction to 40

Mental Math Strategies

Calendar and Time

Numbers to 120

Addition and Subtraction to 100

Getting Ready for Multiplication and Division

Money

Introducing

Math in Focus®

Reteach

Reteach 1A and *1B*, written to complement *Math in Focus®: Singapore Math® by Marshall Cavendish* Grade 1, offer a second opportunity to practice skills and concepts at the entry level. Key vocabulary terms are explained in context, complemented by sample problems with clearly worked solutions.

Not all children are able to master a new concept or skill after the first practice. A second opportunity to practice at the same level before moving on can be key to long-term success.

Monitor students' levels of understanding during daily instruction and as they work on Practice exercises. Provide *Reteach* worksheets for extra support to students who would benefit from further practice at a basic level.

 Weight

Worksheet 1   Comparing Things

Look at the pictures.

1. Circle the object that is lighter.

flower

glass tank

2. Circle the animal that is heavier.

cat

horse

Fill in the blanks with *greater* or *less*.

3. 15 is _____ than 12.

4. 7 is _____ than 20.

Fill in the blanks with *longest* or *shortest*.

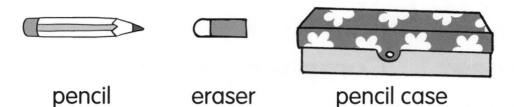

pencil   eraser   pencil case

5.   The eraser is the _____.

6.   The pencil case is the _____.

Look at the pictures.
Then fill in the blanks using the words.

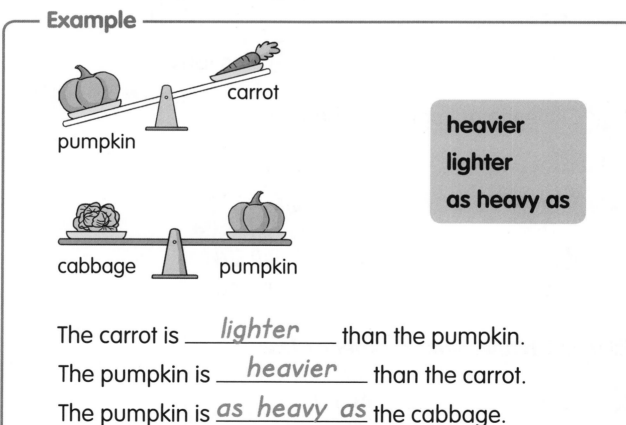

┌─ **Example** ────────────────────────────────

carrot

pumpkin

heavier
lighter
as heavy as

cabbage   pumpkin

The carrot is ___*lighter*___ than the pumpkin.

The pumpkin is ___*heavier*___ than the carrot.

The pumpkin is _*as heavy as*_ the cabbage.

└──

7.

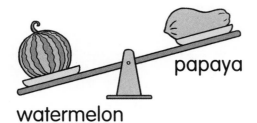

The watermelon is _____ than the papaya.

The papaya is _____ than the watermelon.

8.

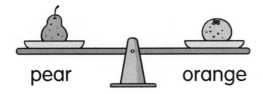

The pear is _____ the orange.

9.

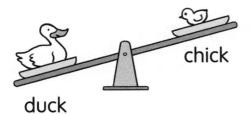

The chick is _____ than the duck.

The duck is _____ than the chick.

10.

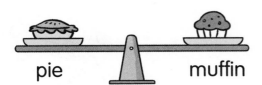

The pie is _____ the muffin.

Fill in the blanks.

> **Example**
>
>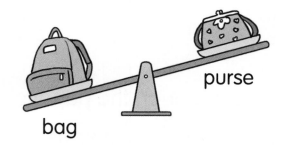
>
> bag   purse
>
>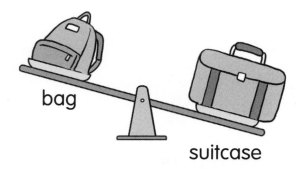
>
> bag   suitcase
>
> The bag is heavier than the ____*purse*____.
>
> The ____*suitcase*____ is heavier than the bag.
>
> So, the ____*suitcase*____ is the **heaviest**.
>
> The purse is lighter than the bag.
> The bag is lighter than the suitcase.
> So, the purse is the **lightest**.
>
>

11.   The _____ is heavier than the cat.

12.   The _____ is heavier than the mouse.

13.   So, the _____ is the heaviest.

14.   The _____ is lighter than the dog.

15.   The _____ is lighter than the cat.

16.   So, the _____ is the lightest.

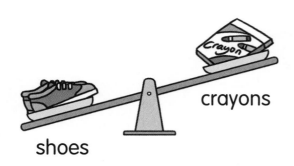

17. The _____ is lighter than the box of crayons.

18. The _____ is lighter than the pair of shoes.

19. So, the _____ is the lightest.

20. The _____ is heavier than the key.

21. The _____ is heavier than the box of crayons.

22. So, the _____ is the heaviest.

Worksheet 2   Finding the Weight of Things

Count.
Write the number in the box.

1.

2.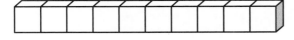

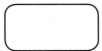

3.

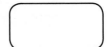

4.

5.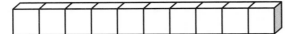

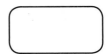

Look at the pictures.
Then fill in the blanks.

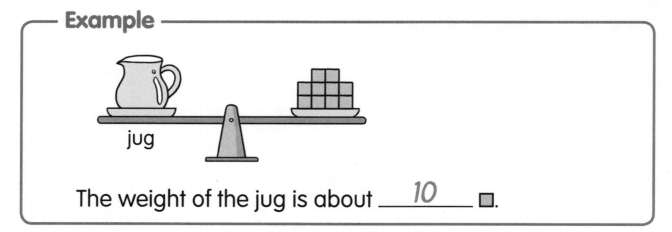

Example

The weight of the jug is about ___*10*___ ☐.

6.

The weight of the doll is about _____ ☐.

7.

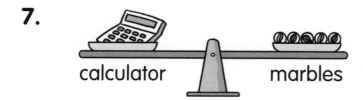

The weight of the calculator is about _____ marbles.

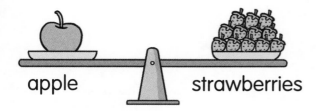
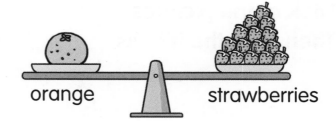

8. The weight of the apple is about _____ strawberries.

9. The weight of the orange is about _____ strawberries.

10. The _____ is heavier than the _____.

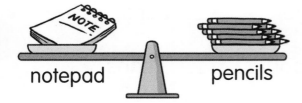
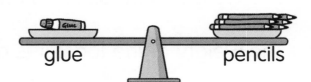

11. The weight of the notepad is about _____ pencils.

12. The weight of the glue is about _____ pencils.

13. The _____ is lighter than the _____.

Look at the pictures.
Then fill in the blanks.

kettle   cans   toaster   cans

cooker   cans

14. The weight of the kettle is about _____ cans.

15. The weight of the toaster is about _____ cans.

16. The weight of the cooker is about _____ cans.

17. The toaster is heavier than the _____.

18. The cooker is heavier than the _____.

19. So, the cooker is heavier than the _____.

20. The _____ is the lightest.

21. The _____ is the heaviest.

Worksheet 3   Finding Weight in Units

Fill in the blanks.

1 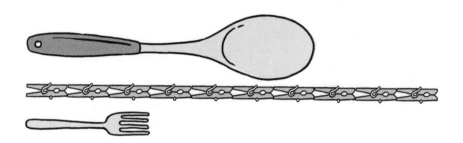 stands for 1 unit.

1.   The fork is about _____ units long.

2.   The ladle is about _____ units long.

Fill in the blanks.

┌─ **Example** ──────────────────────────────────────┐

1 □ stands for 1 **unit**.

alarm clock

> A **unit** is a quantity used for measuring things.

The weight of the alarm clock is ___*11*___ units.

└──┘

3.   1 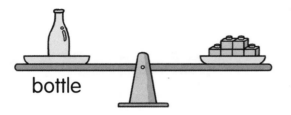 stands for 1 unit.

The weight of the bottle is _____ units.

4.   1 ▯ stands for 1 unit.

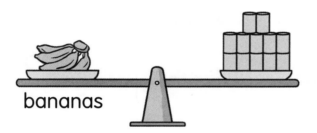

The weight of the bananas is _____ units.

5.   1 ▽ stands for 1 unit.

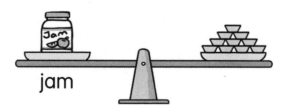

The weight of the jar of jam is _____ units.

Fill in the blanks.

1 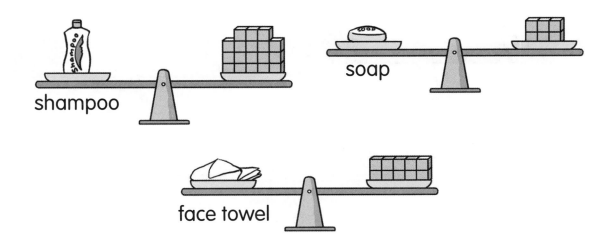 stands for 1 unit.

6. The weight of the shampoo is _____ units.

7. The weight of the soap is _____ units.

8. The weight of the face towel is _____ units.

9. The face towel is lighter than the _____.

10. The face towel is heavier than the _____.

11. The _____ is the lightest.

12. The _____ is the heaviest.

Fill in the blanks.

1 ⊚ stands for 1 unit.

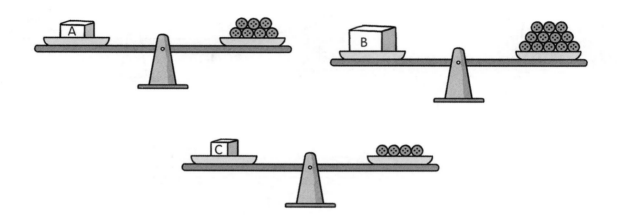

13. The weight of Box A is _____ units.

14. The weight of Box B is _____ units.

15. The weight of Box C is _____ units.

16. Box _____ is the lightest.

17. Box _____ is the heaviest.

18. Arrange the boxes in order from the heaviest to the lightest.

_____, _____, _____
  heaviest   lightest

CHAPTER 11 Picture Graphs and Bar Graphs

Worksheet 1   Simple Picture Graphs

Count.
Write the number.

1.

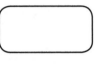

2.

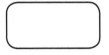

3.

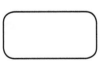

4.

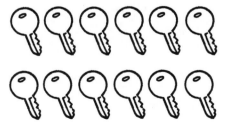

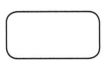

Count.
Circle the set that has more.
Then fill in the blanks.

5.

carrots   eggs

There are _____ carrots.

There are _____ eggs.

There are more _____ than _____.

6.

shells   mushrooms

There are _____ shells.

There are _____ mushrooms.

There are more _____ than _____.

7.

burgers   buns

There are _____ burgers.

There are _____ buns.

There are more _____ than _____.

Count.
Circle the set that has fewer.
Then fill in the blanks.

8.

apples   oranges

There are _____ apples.

There are _____ oranges.

There are fewer _____ than _____.

9.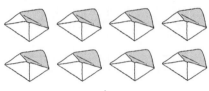

notepads   envelopes

There are _____ notepads.

There are _____ envelopes.

There are fewer _____ than _____.

10.

rabbits   cats

There are _____ rabbits.

There are _____ cats.

There are fewer _____ than _____.

Look at the picture graphs.
Then fill in the blanks.

> **Example**
>
> The picture graph shows the number of buttons that Julia has.
>
> **Julia's Buttons**
>
>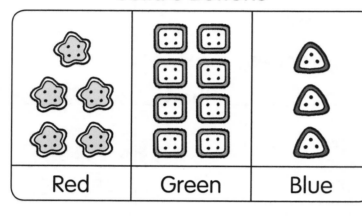
>
> | Red | Green | Blue |
>
> A **picture graph** uses pictures or symbols to show data.
>
> There are ___5___ red buttons.
>
> There are ___8___ green buttons.
>
> There are ___3___ blue buttons.
>
> **Data** is information that has numbers.
>
> There are ___3___ **more** green buttons than red buttons.
>
> There are ___5___ **fewer** blue buttons than green buttons.
>
> Julia has the **most** _green_ buttons.
>
> She has the **fewest** _blue_ buttons.
>
> **Most** means the greatest number.
> **Fewest** means the least number.
>
>

The picture graph shows some animals that can be found at the zoo.

Animals at the Zoo

| Zebra | Elephant | Monkey |

11. There are _____ zebras.

12. There are _____ elephants.

13. There are _____ monkeys.

14. There are fewer _____ than monkeys.

15. There are more _____ than monkeys.

16. The number of _____ is the greatest.

17. The number of _____ is the least.

The picture graph shows the fruits that Mrs. Louis bought from the market.

Fruits Mrs. Louis Bought

18. Mrs. Louis bought _____ apples.

19. She bought _____ pears.

20. She also bought _____ oranges.

21. She bought more _____ than pears.

22. She bought fewer _____ than pears.

23. She bought the greatest number of _____.

24. She bought the least number of _____.

25. She bought _____ fruits in all.

Worksheet 2   More Picture Graphs

Look at the picture graphs.
Then solve.

── **Example** ──

The picture graph shows the ways the students in a class go to school.

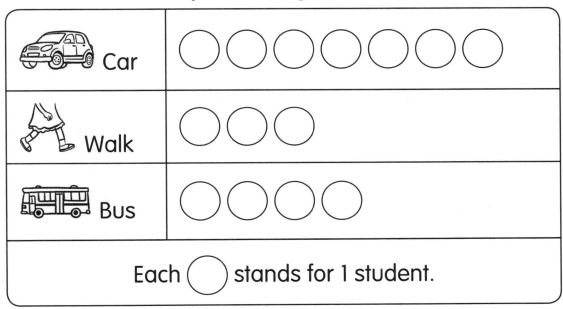

Ways of Going to School

🚗 Car	◯ ◯ ◯ ◯ ◯ ◯ ◯
🚶 Walk	◯ ◯ ◯
🚌 Bus	◯ ◯ ◯ ◯

Each ◯ stands for 1 student.

_____*3*_____ students walk to school.

_____*7*_____ students go to school by car.

_____*4*_____ students go to school by bus.

More students go to school by ___*car*___ than by bus.

The least number of students ___*walk*___ to school.

There are ___*14*___ students in the class in all.

The picture graph shows the number of ribbons Leigh has.

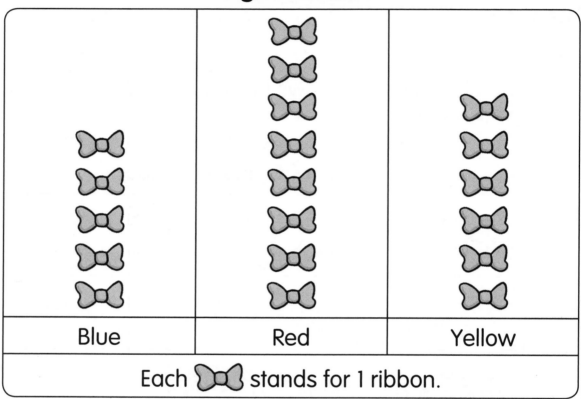

Leigh's Ribbons

| Blue | Red | Yellow |

Each 🎀 stands for 1 ribbon.

1. Leigh has _____ yellow ribbons.

2. She has _____ red ribbons.

3. She has _____ blue ribbons.

4. Leigh has more yellow ribbons than _____ ribbons.

5. She has _____ fewer blue ribbons than red ribbons.

6. The number of _____ ribbons is the least.

7. She has _____ ribbons in all.

The picture graph shows the pets that are in a pet shop.

Pets in a Pet Shop

Bird	★ ★ ★ ★ ★ ★ ★
Puppy	★ ★ ★ ★ ★ ★ ★ ★ ★ ★ ★ ★
Hamster	★ ★ ★ ★ ★ ★ ★ ★
Kitten	★ ★ ★ ★ ★ ★ ★

Each ★ stands for 1 pet.

8. How many kittens are there in the shop? _____

9. How many hamsters are there in the shop? _____

10. How many birds are there in the shop? _____

11. There are fewer _____ than hamsters.

12. There are _____ more puppies than hamsters.

13. The number of _____ is the greatest.

14. There are equal numbers of _____ and

_____.

The picture graph shows the number of storybooks that five children read in a month.

Number of Storybooks Read in a Month

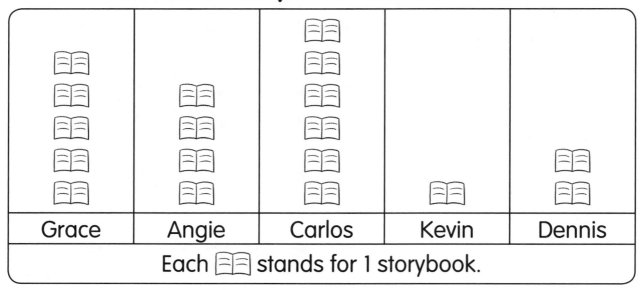

15. How many storybooks did each child read?

Grace: _____   Angie: _____   Carlos: _____

Kevin: _____   Dennis: _____

16. Dennis read more storybooks than _____.

17. _____ read the greatest number of storybooks.

18. Who read the least number of storybooks? _____

19. The children read _____ storybooks in all.

Worksheet 3   Tally Charts and Bar Graphs

Look at the pictures.
Then complete the tally chart.

── Example ──

Sea Animal	Tally	Number
Octopus	////	4
Crab	~~////~~ /	6
Seahorse	~~////~~ ~~////~~ /	11

A **tally chart** is a quick way of counting the data in each category.

I draw 4 **tally marks** like this ////.
To show 5 tally marks, I draw the fifth mark across the 4 tally marks. ~~////~~

1.

Fruit	Tally	Number
Cherry		
Strawberry		
Banana		

2.

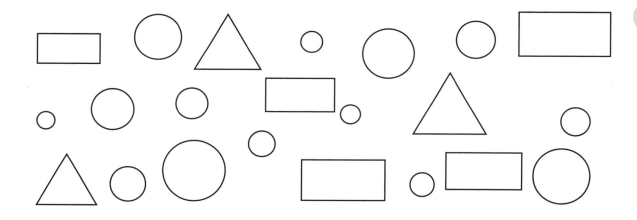

Shape	Tally	Number
Rectangle		
Circle		
Triangle		

Complete the tally charts.
Then complete the bar graphs.

Example

Sports	Tally	Number
Basketball	$\cancel{||||}$ |||	8
Football	$\cancel{||||}$ $\cancel{||||}$	10
Volleyball	|||	3

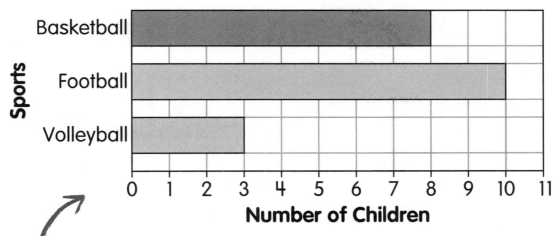

Favorite Sports

A **bar graph** uses the lengths of bars and a scale to show the data.

3.

School Supplies	Tally	Number
Book		5
File	‖‖‖ ‖	
Pencil	‖‖‖	

School Supplies Emelda Bought

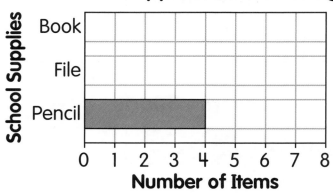

4.

Flower	Tally	Number
Rose	‖	
Lily	‖‖‖ ‖	
Daisy	‖‖‖	

Flowers Sold at a Florist

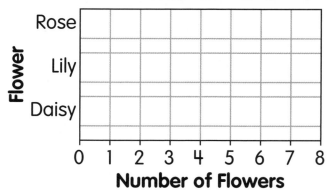

Chad has some toys in his toy box.
The tally chart shows the different toys he has in his toy box.
Complete the tally chart.

5.

Toy	Tally	Number
Toy boat	ЖЖ ЖЖ	
Toy car	ЖЖ	
Building blocks	ЖЖ |||	

Make a bar graph.

6.

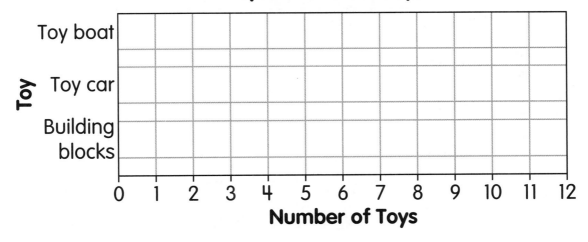

Fill in the blanks.

7.   Chad has the most _____.

8.   He has the fewest _____.

9.   He has _____ toy cars and toy boats in all.

The tally chart shows the favorite fruit juices of some children.
Complete the tally chart.

10.

Fruit Juice	Tally	Number
Orange	卌 卌	
Cranberry	////	
Grape	卌 //	
Apple	////	

Make a bar graph.

11.

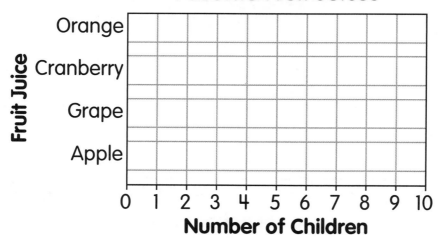

Favorite Fruit Juices

Fill in the blanks.

12. The same number of children like _____ and _____ juice.

13. How many fewer children like grape juice than orange juice? _____

CHAPTER 12 Numbers to 40

Worksheet 1   Counting to 40

Match.

1.

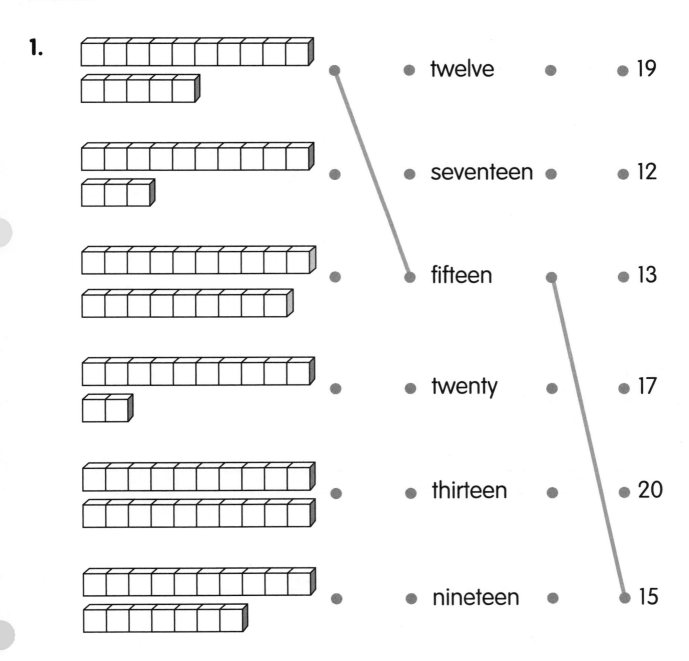

twelve   19

seventeen   12

fifteen   13

twenty   17

thirteen   20

nineteen   15

Fill in the blanks.

2.

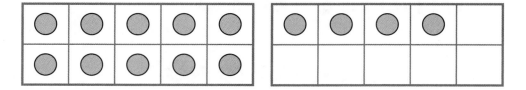

14 is _____ and _____.

10 and 4 make _____.

10 + _____ = 14

3.

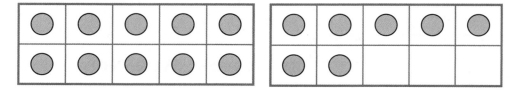

17 is _____ and _____.

10 and 7 make _____.

10 + _____ = 17

Count on.
Fill in the blanks.

┌─ **Example** ─────────────────────────────────┐

10   20 21 22

10, ... __*20*__, __*21*__, __*22*__

There are __*22*__ ☐.

└───┘

4.

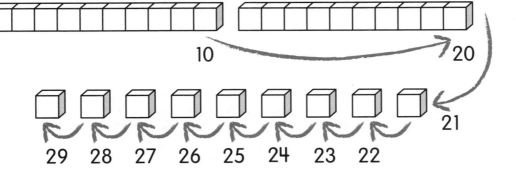

10, ... 20, _____, _____, _____,

twenty-one   twenty-two   twenty-three

_____, _____, _____,

twenty-four   twenty-five   twenty-six

_____, _____, _____,

twenty-seven   twenty-eight   twenty-nine

There are _____ ⬜.

5.

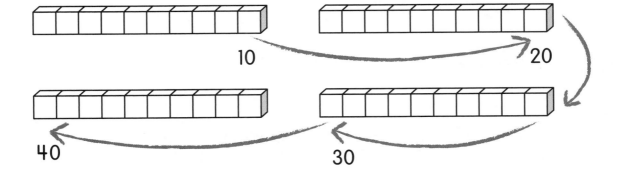

10, ... 20, ... _____, ... _____

thirty   forty

There are _____ ⬜.

Count on.
Fill in the blanks.

6.

There are _____ yo-yos.

7.

There are _____ gifts.

8.

There are _____ tarts.

Write the numbers.

9.   twenty-four _____   **10.**   thirty _____

11.   twenty-one _____   **12.**   twenty-eight _____

13.   thirty-three _____   **14.**   thirty-seven _____

15.   thirty-five _____   **16.**   twenty-nine _____

17.   forty _____   **18.**   thirty-one _____

Match.

19.

27 ●   ● thirty-nine

32 ●   ● twenty-two

39 ●   ● forty

25 ●   ● thirty-six

34 ●   ● thirty-two

22 ●   ● twenty-seven

40 ●   ● thirty-four

36 ●   ● twenty-five

Fill in the blanks.

Example

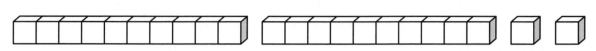

There are __*22*__ 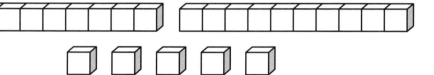.

Twenty and __*two*__ make twenty-two.

__*20*__ + 2 = __*22*__

20.

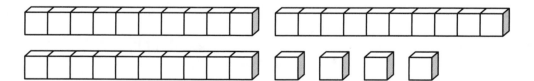

There are _____ ⬜.

Twenty and _____ make twenty-five.

_____ + 5 = _____

21.

There are _____ ⬜.

Thirty and _____ make thirty-four.

_____ + 4 = _____

Worksheet 2   Place Value

Read the place-value chart.
Find the missing numbers.

1.

Tens	Ones
1	1

11 is _____ ten _____ one.

11 = _____ + _____

2.

Tens	Ones
1	6

16 is _____ ten _____ ones.

16 = _____ + _____

Circle groups of 10.
Count on.
Then fill in the place-value charts.

Example

Tens	Ones
2	3

3.

Tens	Ones

4.

Tens	Ones

5.

Tens	Ones

6.

Tens	Ones

Complete each place-value chart.
Then write the number.

Example

Tens	Ones
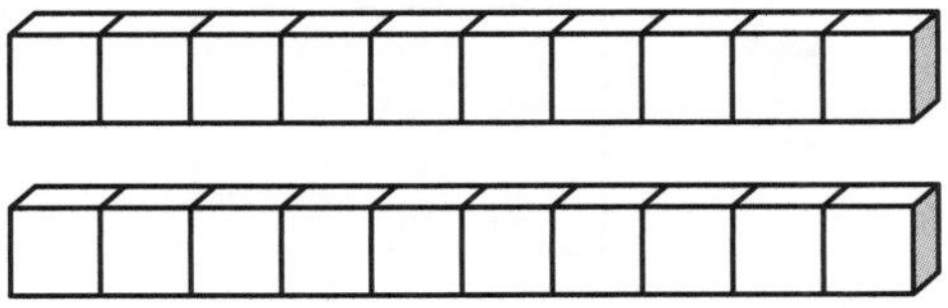	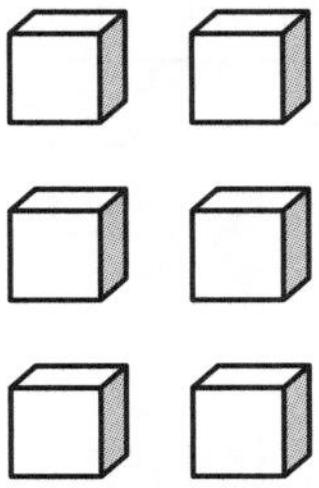
2	6

26

7.

Tens	Ones
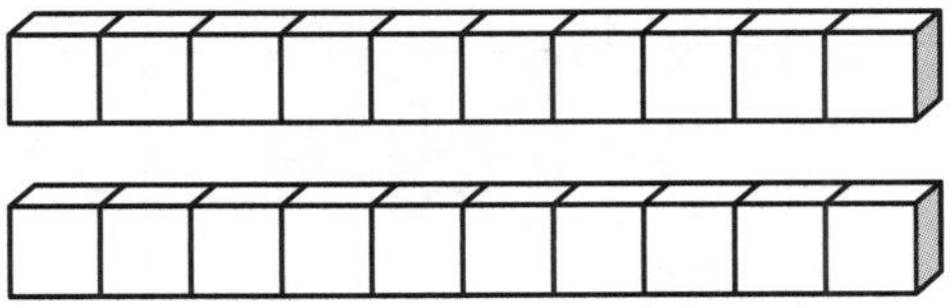	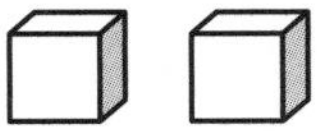

8.

Tens	Ones
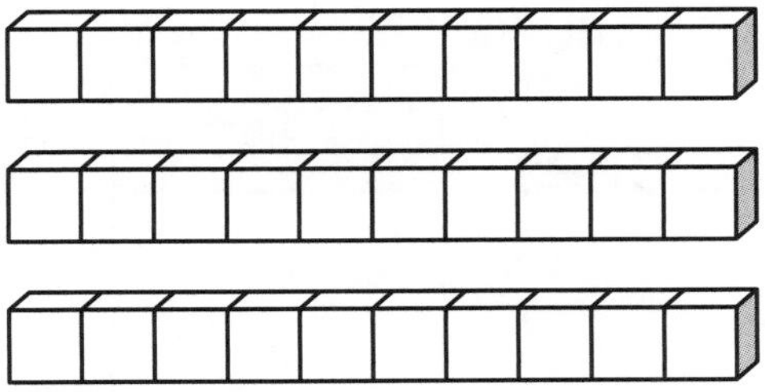	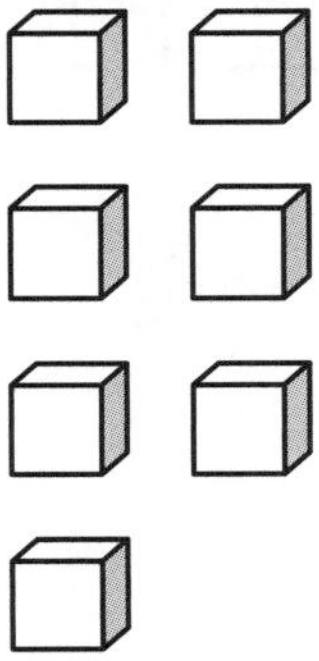

Name: _____ **Date:** _____

Count in tens and ones.
Fill in the missing numbers in the place-value charts and blanks.

Example

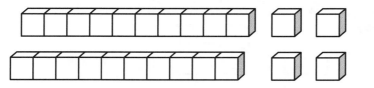

Tens	Ones
2	4

24 = ____2____ tens ____4____ ones

20 + 4 = ____24____

9.

Tens	Ones

30 = _____ tens _____ ones

30 + 0 = _____

10.

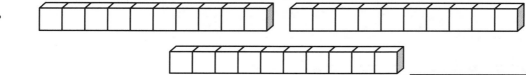

Tens	Ones

33 = _____ tens _____ ones

30 + 3 = _____

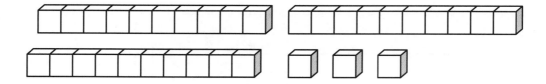

Worksheet 3 Comparing, Ordering, and Patterns

Compare and order.
Fill in the blanks with these numbers.

(15)   (19)   (12)

1. _____ is greater than 15.

2. _____ is less than 15.

3. _____ is the greatest number.

4. _____ is the least number.

5. Order the numbers from <u>greatest</u> to <u>least</u>.

_____, _____, _____
greatest   least

Complete the number pattern by counting on.

6.   10, 12, _____, 16, _____, 20

Complete the number pattern by counting back.

7.   _____, 15, _____, 11, 9, _____

Count on or count back.
Then fill in the blanks.
Use the counting tape to help you.

Example

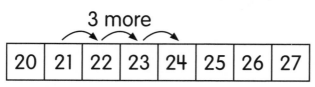

_____24_____ is 3 more than 21.

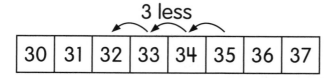

_____32_____ is 3 less than 35.

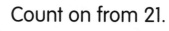Count on from 21.

Count back from 35.

8.

| 25 | 26 | 27 | 28 | 29 | 30 | 31 | 32 |

_____ is 2 more than 27.

9.

| 28 | 29 | 30 | 31 | 32 | 33 | 34 | 35 | 36 | 37 | 38 | 39 | 40 |

_____ is 8 more than 30.

10.

| 32 | 33 | 34 | 35 | 36 | 37 | 38 | 39 | 40 |

3 more than 36 is _____.

11.

| 20 | 21 | 22 | 23 | 24 | 25 | 26 | 27 | 28 | 29 | 30 |

_____ is 7 less than 29.

12.

| 28 | 29 | 30 | 31 | 32 | 33 | 34 | 35 |

_____ is 5 less than 34.

13.

| 30 | 31 | 32 | 33 | 34 | 35 | 36 | 37 | 38 | 39 | 40 |

9 less than 40 is _____.

Complete the place-value charts.
Compare.
Then fill in the blanks.

Example

	Tens	Ones
30	3	0

	Tens	Ones
25	2	5

_____30_____ is greater than _____25_____.
_____25_____ is less than _____30_____.

> Compare the tens.
> The tens are different.
> 3 tens is greater than 2 tens.

14.

	Tens	Ones
32		

	Tens	Ones
27		

_____ is greater than _____.

_____ is less than _____.

15.

Tens	Ones

23

Tens	Ones

36

_____ is greater than _____.

_____ is less than _____.

16.

Tens	Ones

28

Tens	Ones

21

_____ is greater than _____.

_____ is less than _____.

17.

Tens	Ones

34

Tens	Ones

37

_____ is greater than _____.

_____ is less than _____.

Compare the tens.
Are the tens equal?
Compare the ones.
Are the ones equal?

Name: _____   Date: _____

Count the  in each set.
Write the numbers in the boxes.
Then fill in the blanks.

Example

Set A

26

Set B

31

Which set has more? Set ____B____

Which number is greater?

____31____ is greater than ____26____.

18.

Set A

Set B

Which set has more? Set _____

Which number is greater?

_____ is greater than _____.

19. Set A

Set B

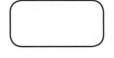

Which set has more? Set _____

Which number is greater?

_____ is greater than _____.

20. Set A

Set B

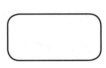

Which set has fewer? Set _____

Which number is less?

_____ is less than _____.

21. Set A

Set B

Which set has fewer? Set _____

Which number is less?

_____ is less than _____.

Compare.
Use place value to help you.
Write the number that is greater in the box.

22. 25 or 36  **23.** 32 or 21

Write the number that is less in the box.

24. 40 or 27  **25.** 29 or 34

Compare the numbers.
Use place-value charts to help you.
Fill in the blanks.
Then order the numbers.

--- Example ---

Compare 24, 35, and 28.

Tens	Ones
2	4

Tens	Ones
3	5

Tens	Ones
2	8

_____35_____ is the greatest number.

_____24_____ is the least number.

_____24_____, _____28_____, _____35_____
  least   greatest

26. Compare 23, 36, and 31.

_____ is the greatest number.

_____ is the least number.

_____, _____, _____
   least   greatest

27. Compare 28, 35, and 20.

_____ is the greatest number.

_____ is the least number.

_____, _____, _____
  greatest   least

28. Compare 40, 25, and 34.

_____ is the greatest number.

_____ is the least number.

_____, _____, _____
  greatest   least

Complete each number pattern.

Example

$+1$ $+1$ $+1$ $+1$

32, 33, ___*34*___, ___*35*___, 36, ___*37*___, 38, ___*39*___

29. 24, _____, _____, 27, 28, _____, 30

30. _____, 32, 31, _____, _____, 28, _____

31. 22, 25, _____, 31, _____, 37, _____

32. 34, _____, 30, _____, 26, 24, _____

33. 20, 24, _____, 32, _____, 40

34. _____, _____, 30, 26, _____, 18

CHAPTER 13 Addition and Subtraction to 40

Worksheet 1   Addition Without Regrouping

Complete the number bonds.
Then add.

1.   9 + 5 = _____

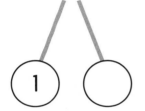

2.   6 + 7 = _____

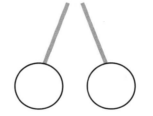

3.   12 + 2 = _____

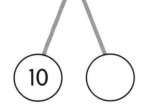

4.   15 + 4 = _____

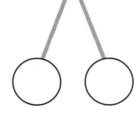

Find the related addition facts.

5.   7 – 3 = 4   _____ + _____ = _____

6.   13 – 8 = 5   _____ + _____ = _____

7.   15 – 6 = 9   _____ + _____ = _____

Name: _____ **Date:** _____

Add by counting on.

> **Example**
>
> Find 24 + 4.
>
>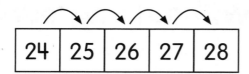
>
> | 24 | 25 | 26 | 27 | 28 |
> |----|----|----|----|----|
>
> 24, _25_, _26_, _27_, _28_
>
> 24 + 4 = _28_

Count on from the greater number.

8. Find 20 + 5.

20	21	22	23	24	25

20, _____, _____, _____, _____, _____

20 + 5 = _____

9. Find 31 + 6.

31	32	33	34	35	36	37

31, _____, _____, _____, _____, _____, _____

31 + 6 = _____

10. Find 32 + 7.

32	33	34	35	36	37	38	39

32, _____, _____, _____, _____, _____, _____,

_____

32 + 7 = _____

Complete each place-value chart.
Then add.

Example

Find 27 + 2.

```
    Tens    Ones
     2       7
+            2
    _____
     2       9
```

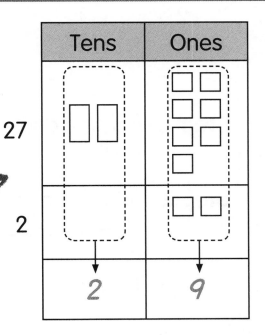

place-value chart

27

2

Step 1 Add the ones.
7 + 2 = 9

Step 2 Add the tens.
20 + 0 = 20

So, 27 + 2 = __29__.

---

11. Find 21 + 4.

Tens	Ones
2	1
+	4

Step 1 Add the ones.
1 + 4 = _____

Step 2 Add the tens.
20 + 0 = _____

So, 21 + 4 = _____.

	Tens	Ones
21		
4		

12. Find 23 + 3.

Tens	Ones
2	3
+	3

Step 1 Add the ones.
3 + 3 = _____

Step 2 Add the tens.
20 + 0 = _____

So, 23 + 3 = _____.

	Tens	Ones
23		
3		

13. Find 33 + 5.

	Tens	Ones

Tens   Ones
  3   3   33
+ _____ 5
_____

                  5

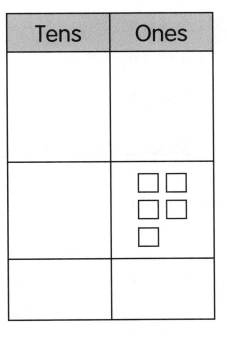

Step 1 Add the ones.

_____ + _____ = _____

Step 2 Add the tens.

_____ + _____ = _____

So, 33 + 5 = _____.

14. Find 31 + 8.

	Tens	Ones

Tens   Ones
  3   1   31
+ _____ 8
_____

                  8

Step 1 Add the ones.

_____ + _____ = _____

Step 2 Add the tens.

_____ + _____ = _____

So, 31 + 8 = _____.

Add.

Name: _____   Date: _____

Example

	Tens	Ones
	3	0
+		7
	3	7

Step 1 $0 + 7 =$ __7__

Step 2 $30 + 0 =$ __30__

So, $30 + 7 =$ __37__.

15.

Step 1 $5 + 4 =$ _____

Step 2 $20 + 0 =$ _____

So, $25 + 4 =$ _____.

	Tens	Ones
	2	5
+		4

16.

Step 1 _____ $+$ _____ $=$ _____

Step 2 _____ $+$ _____ $=$ _____

So, $32 + 3 =$ _____.

	Tens	Ones
	3	2
+		3

17.

	2	3
+		2

18.

	3	7
+		1

Complete each place-value chart.
Then add.

Example

Find 23 + 11.

```
   Tens      Ones
     2         3
 +   1         1
 ─────────────────
     3         4
```

	Tens	Ones
23	□□	□ □ □
11	□	□
	3	4

Step 1 Add the ones.
3 + 1 = 4

Step 2 Add the tens.
20 + 10 = 30

So, 23 + 11 = __34__.

---

19. Find 15 + 24.

Tens	Ones
1	5
+ 2	4

	Tens	Ones
15	▯	▢▢ ▢▢ ▢
24	▯▯	▢▢ ▢▢

Step 1   Add the ones.
5 + 4 = _____

Step 2   Add the tens.
10 + 20 = _____

So, 15 + 24 = _____.

20. Find 13 + 21.

Tens	Ones
1	3
+ 2	1

	Tens	Ones
13	▯	▢▢ ▢
21		

Step 1   Add the ones.
3 + 1 = _____

Step 2   Add the tens.
10 + 20 = _____

So, 13 + 21 = _____.

21.   Find 30 + 10.

	Tens	Ones
30		
10	☐	

Tens   Ones
   3   0
+ 1   0
_____

Step 1   Add the ones.

_____ + _____ = _____

Step 2   Add the tens.

_____ + _____ = _____

So, 30 + 10 = _____.

22.   Find 20 + 17.

	Tens	Ones
20		
17		

Tens   Ones
   2   0
+ 1   7
_____

Step 1   Add the ones.

_____ + _____ = _____

Step 2   Add the tens.

_____ + _____ = _____

So, 20 + 17 = _____.

Add.

Example

Step 1 6 + 2 = __8__

Step 2 20 + 10 = __30__

So, 26 + 12 = __38__.

	Tens	Ones
	2	6
+	1	2
	3	8

23. **Step 1** 9 + 0 = _____

Step 2 10 + 20 = _____

So, 19 + 20 = _____.

	Tens	Ones
	1	9
+	2	0

24. **Step 1** _____ + _____ = _____

Step 2 _____ + _____ = _____

So, _____ + _____ = _____.

	Tens	Ones
	2	2
+	1	4

25.
```
   1     5
+  1     2
_____
```

26.
```
   2     1
+  1     6
_____
```

Worksheet 2   Addition with Regrouping

Regroup the ones into tens and ones.
Then complete the place-value chart.

— Example —

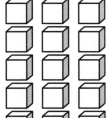 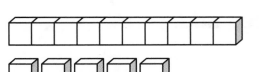

> **Regroup** means to
> change 10 ones for 1 ten.

Tens	Ones		Tens	Ones
	15	=	1	5

1.

Tens	Ones		Tens	Ones
	18	=		

2.

Tens	Ones		Tens	Ones
	21	=	2	

3.

Tens	Ones
	25

=

Tens	Ones

Complete each place-value chart.
Then add.

┌─ **Example** ───┐

Find 14 + 7.

Tens	Ones
1̇	4
+	7
2	**1**

	Tens	Ones
14	□	□ □ □ □
7		□ □ □ □ □ □
	2	**1**

Step 1   Add the ones.
4 + 7 = 11

Regroup the ones.
11 ones = 1 ten 1 one

Step 2   Add the tens.
10 + 10 + 0 = 20

So, 14 + 7 = ___21___.

└──┘

4. Find 19 + 5.

Tens	Ones
1	9
+	5

Tens	Ones
	□ □
□	□ □
	□ □
	□ □
	□

19

Step 1 Add the ones.

9 + 5 = _____

Regroup the ones.

_____ ones = 1 ten 4 ones

5

Step 2 Add the tens.

10 + 10 + 0 = _____

So, 19 + 5 = _____.

5. Find 26 + 8.

Tens	Ones
2	6
+	8

Tens	Ones

26

Step 1 Add the ones.

_____ + _____ = _____

Regroup the ones.

_____ ones = _____ ten

. _____ ones

	□ □
	□ □
	□ □
	□ □

8

Step 2 Add the tens.

_____ + _____ + _____ = _____

So, 26 + 8 = _____.

Add.

┌─ **Example** ──┐

Step 1 $9 + 3 =$ ___12___

Regroup the ones.
12 ones = 1 ten 2 ones

	Tens	Ones
	$\overset{1}{2}$	9
+		3
	3	2

Step 2 $10 + 20 + 0 =$ ___30___

So, $29 + 3 =$ ___32___.

└──┘

6.   **Step 1** $3 + 7 =$ _____

Regroup the ones.
_____ ones = 1 ten 0 ones

	Tens	Ones
	3	3
+		7

Step 2 $10 + 30 + 0 =$ _____

So, $33 + 7 =$ _____.

7.   **Step 1** $7 + 4 =$ _____

Regroup the ones.
_____ ones = _____ ten
_____ one

	Tens	Ones
	2	7
+		4

Step 2 _____ + _____ + _____ = _____

So, $27 + 4 =$ _____.

8.

```
       1    7
  +         3
  _____
```

9.

```
       1    6
  +         8
  _____
```

Complete each place-value chart.
Then add.

--- Example ---

Find 15 + 15.

```
  Tens    Ones
    1
    1      5
  + 1      5
  _____
    3      0
```

	Tens	Ones
15	□	□□□ □□
15	□	□□□ □□
	3	0

Step 1 Add the ones.
5 + 5 = 10.

Regroup the ones.
10 ones = 1 ten 0 ones

Step 2 Add the tens.
10 + 10 + 10 = 30

So, 15 + 15 = __30__.

10. Find 12 + 19.

	Tens	Ones
	1	2
+	1	9

	Tens	Ones
12	☐	☐ ☐
19		

Step 1 Add the ones.
2 + 9 = ____.

Regroup the ones.
____ ones = 1 ten 1 one

Step 2 Add the tens.
10 + 10 + 10 = ____

So, 12 + 19 = ____.

11. Find 16 + 18.

	Tens	Ones
	1	6
+	1	8

	Tens	Ones
16		
18	☐	☐ ☐ ☐ ☐ ☐ ☐ ☐ ☐

Step 1 Add the ones.
____ + ____ = ____.

Regroup the ones.
____ ones = ____ ten ____ ones

Step 2 Add the tens.
____ + ____ + ____ = ____

So, 16 + 18 = ____.

Add.

Example

Step 1 4 + 9 = __13__

Regroup the ones.
13 ones = 1 ten 3 ones

Step 2 10 + 10 + 10 = __30__

So, 14 + 19 = __33__.

	Tens	Ones
	1	4
+	1	9
	3	3

---

12. **Step 1** 7 + 3 = _____

Regroup the ones.
_____ ones = 1 ten 0 ones

Step 2 10 + 20 + 10 = _____

So, 27 + 13 = _____.

	Tens	Ones
	2	7
+	1	3

---

13. **Step 1** _____ + _____ = _____

Regroup the ones.
_____ ones = _____ ten
_____ ones

Step 2 _____ + _____ + _____ = _____

So, 17 + 15 = _____.

	Tens	Ones
	1	7
+	1	5

14.

Tens	Ones
1	9
+ 1	3

15.

Tens	Ones
1	2
+ 2	8

16.

1	6
+ 1	5

17.

1	4
+ 1	8

Worksheet 3   Subtraction Without Regrouping

Complete the number bonds.
Then subtract.

1.   19 – 7 = _____

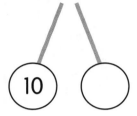

2.   18 – 4 = _____

3.   11 – 5 = _____

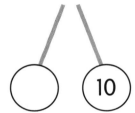

4.   13 – 6 = _____

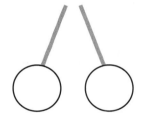

Find the related subtraction facts.

5.   4 + 6 = 10   ➡   _____ – _____ = _____

6.   9 + 8 = 17   ➡   _____ – _____ = _____

7.   5 + 9 = 14   ➡   _____ – _____ = _____

Subtract by counting back.

┌─ **Example** ───┐

Find 28 – 6.

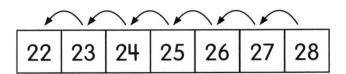

| 22 | 23 | 24 | 25 | 26 | 27 | 28 |

28, _27_, _26_, _25_, _24_, _23_, _22_

28 – 6 = _22_

Count back from the greater number.

└──┘

8. Find 25 – 4.

| 21 | 22 | 23 | 24 | 25 |

25, _____, _____, _____, _____

25 – 4 = _____

9. Find 34 – 2.

| 32 | 33 | 34 |

34, _____, _____

34 – 2 = _____

10. Find 38 – 5.

| 33 | 34 | 35 | 36 | 37 | 38 |

38, _____, _____, _____, _____, _____

38 – 5 = _____

Complete each place-value chart.
Then subtract.

— Example —

Find 19 – 7.

Tens	Ones
1	9
–	7
1	*2*

	Tens	Ones
19	☐	⊠ ⊠ ⊠ ⊠ ⊠ ⊠ ⊠ ☐ ☐
	1	*2*

Step 1 Subtract the ones.
9 – 7 = 2

Step 2 Subtract the tens.
10 – 0 = 10

So, 19 – 7 = __*12*__.

11. Find 24 – 4.

Tens	Ones
2	4
–	4

	Tens	Ones
24	☐ ☐	☐ ☐ ☐ ☐

Step 1 Subtract the ones.
4 – 4 = _____

Step 2 Subtract the tens.
20 – 0 = _____

So, 24 – 4 = _____.

12. Find 28 − 5.

Tens	Ones
2	8
−	5

28

Tens	Ones

Step 1 Subtract the ones.
8 − 5 = _____

Step 2 Subtract the tens.
20 − 0 = _____

So, 28 − 5 = _____.

13. Find 36 − 3.

Tens	Ones
3	6
−	3

36

Tens	Ones

Step 1 Subtract the ones.
_____ − _____ = _____

Step 2 Subtract the tens.
_____ − _____ = _____

So, 36 − 3 = _____.

Subtract.

Example

Step 1 5 – 5 = ___0___

Step 2 30 – 0 = ___30___

So, 35 – 5 = ___30___.

Tens	Ones
3	5
–	5
3	0

---

14. **Step 1** 9 – 8 = _____

    Step 2 20 – 0 = _____

    So, 29 – 8 = _____.

Tens	Ones
2	9
–	8

15. **Step 1** _____ – _____ = _____

    Step 2 _____ – _____ = _____

    So, 37 – 4 = _____.

Tens	Ones
3	7
–	4

16.

Tens	Ones
3	9
–	6

17.

Tens	Ones
2	7
–	3

18.

2	5
–	5

19.

3	6
–	4

Complete each place-value chart.
Then subtract.

Example

Find 25 – 13.

```
     Tens      Ones
      2         5
  –   1         3
  _____
      1         2
```

Tens	Ones
25 ☐☒	☒☒ ☒☐ ☐
1	2

Step 1 Subtract the ones.
5 – 3 = 2

Step 2 Subtract the tens.
20 – 10 = 10

So, 25 – 13 = __12__.

---

20. Find 29 – 14.

```
     Tens      Ones
      2         9
  –   1         4
  _____
```

Tens	Ones
29 ☐☐	☐☐☐ ☐☐☐ ☐☐☐

Step 1 Subtract the ones.
9 – 4 = _____

Step 2 Subtract the tens.
20 – 10 = _____

So, 29 – 14 = _____.

21. Find 37 − 16.

Tens	Ones
3	7
− 1	6

37

Tens	Ones

Step 1 Subtract the ones.
7 − 6 = _____

Step 2 Subtract the tens.
30 − 10 = _____

So, 37 − 16 = _____.

22. Find 32 − 20.

Tens	Ones
3	2
− 2	0

32

Tens	Ones

Step 1 Subtract the ones.
_____ − _____ = _____

Step 2 Subtract the tens.
_____ − _____ = _____

So, 32 − 20 = _____.

Subtract.

Example

Step 1 8 − 4 = _4_

Step 2 30 − 10 = _20_

So, 38 − 14 = _24_.

Tens	Ones
3	8
− 1	4
2	4

---

23. **Step 1** 4 − 0 = _____

Step 2 20 − 10 = _____

So, 24 − 10 = _____.

Tens	Ones
2	4
− 1	0

---

24. **Step 1** _____ − _____ = _____

Step 2 _____ − _____ = _____

So, 36 − 23 = _____.

Tens	Ones
3	6
− 2	3

25.

Tens	Ones
3	4
− 2	1

26.

Tens	Ones
2	8
− 1	6

27.

4	0
− 2	0

28.

3	5
− 1	2

Worksheet 4   Subtraction with Regrouping

Regroup the tens into tens and ones.
Then complete the place-value chart.

Example

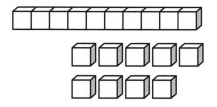 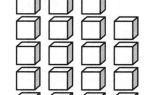

Tens	Ones
1	9

=

Tens	Ones
	19

1.

Tens	Ones
2	4

=

Tens	Ones
1	

2.

Tens	Ones
3	3

=

Tens	Ones
2	

3.

Tens	Ones
3	7

=

Tens	Ones

Subtract.
Use the place-value chart to help you.

Example

Find 35 – 16.

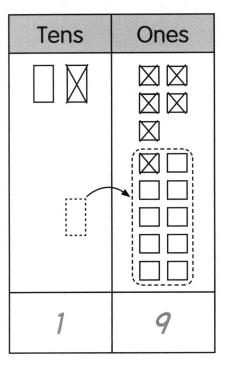

Tens   Ones

$$\begin{array}{cc}
\overset{2}{\cancel{3}} & {}^{1}5 \\
-\;\; 1 & 6 \\
\hline
1 & 9
\end{array}$$

35

Step 1   Subtract the ones.

Regroup the tens and
ones in 35.
35 = 3 tens 5 ones
    = 2 tens 15 ones
15 – 6 = 9

Step 2   Subtract the tens.
20 – 10 = 10

So, 35 – 16 = ___19___.

---

4. Find 34 − 18.

	Tens	Ones

Tens   Ones

  ²
  3̶   ¹4

−   1   8
_____

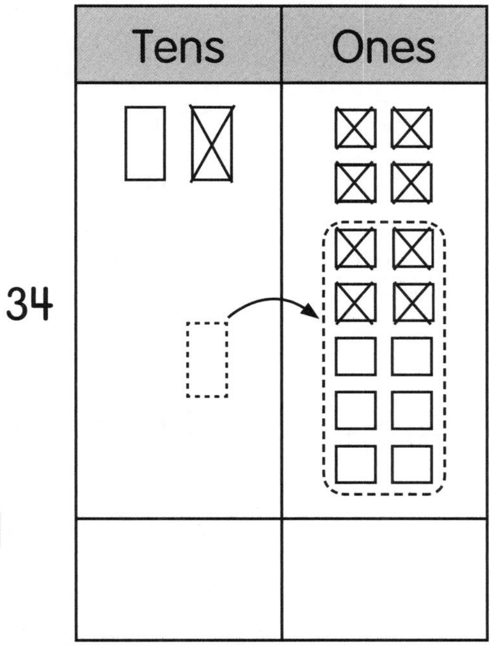

Step 1 Subtract the ones.

Regroup the tens and
ones in 34.
34 = 3 tens 4 ones
   = 2 tens 14 ones
14 − 8 = _____

Step 2 Subtract the tens.
20 − 10 = _____

So, 34 − 18 = _____.

5. Find 23 – 17.

Tens	Ones
2	3
– 1	7

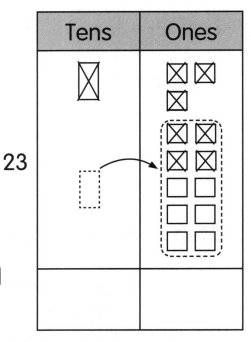

23

Step 1 Subtract the ones.

Regroup the tens and ones in 23.
23 = 2 tens 3 ones
= 1 ten 13 ones

13 – 7 = _____

Step 2 Subtract the tens.
10 – 10 = _____

So, 23 – 17 = _____.

6. **Step 1**   Subtract the ones.

Regroup the tens and ones in 36.
3 tens 6 ones = 2 tens

_____ ones

_____ – _____ = _____

Tens	Ones
3	6
– 1	7

Step 2   Subtract the tens.

_____ – _____ = _____

So, 36 – 17 = _____.

Regroup and subtract.

Example

Tens	Ones
$\overset{1}{\cancel{2}}$	$^1 3$
–	8
1	5

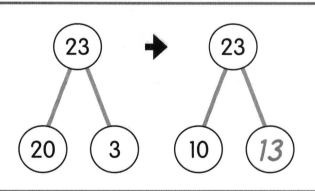

7.

Tens	Ones
2	6
–	9

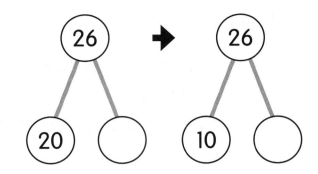

8.

Tens	Ones
3	4
–	7

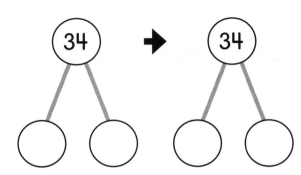

Subtract.

9.

Tens	Ones
$\overset{1}{\cancel{2}}$	$^1 1$
–	5

10.

Tens	Ones
2	5
–	8

11.

3	0
–	4

12.

3	3
–	6

Regroup and subtract.

Example

Tens	Ones
2	6
− 1	8
	8

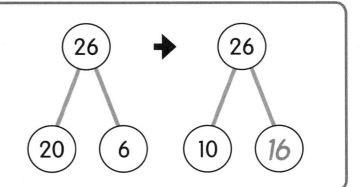

13.

Tens	Ones
2	2
− 1	7

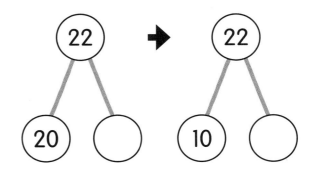

14.

Tens	Ones
3	1
− 1	3

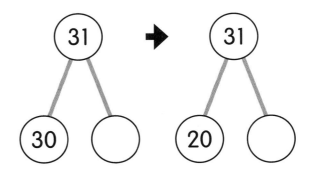

15.

Tens	Ones
3	5
− 2	9

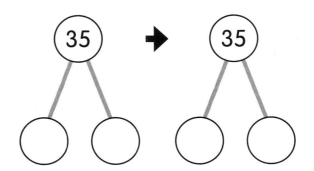

Subtract.

16.   2   4
       – 1   5
       _____

17.   2   7
       – 1   9
       _____

18.   3   3
       – 1   4
       _____

19.   4   0
       – 2   1
       _____

Worksheet 5 Adding Three Numbers

Complete the number bonds.
Make ten.
Then add.

Example

5 + 7 + 4 = ___16___

⑤ ② ⑩

5 + ___5___ = 10

___2___ + 4 = 6

___10___ + ___6___ = 16

So, 5 + 7 + 4 = ___16___.

1.   8 + 9 + 3 = _____

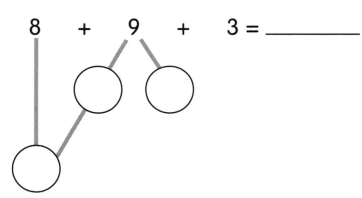

8 + _____ = 10

_____ + 3 = 10

_____ + _____ = 20

So, 8 + 9 + 3 = _____.

2.   7   +   5   +   2 = _____

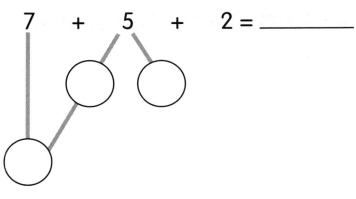

7 + _____ = 10

_____ + 2 = 4

_____ + _____ = 14

So, _____ + _____ + _____ = _____.

3.   6   +   8   +   4 = _____

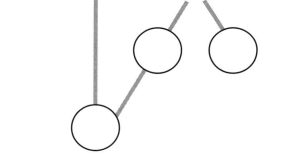

8 + _____ = 10

6 + _____ = 8

_____ + _____ = _____

So, _____ + _____ + _____ = _____.

Add.

4.   9 + 2 + 5 = _____   **5.**   4 + 8 + 9 = _____

Worksheet 6   Real-World Problems: Addition and Subtraction

Solve.

1. Paulo used 11 shapes to make a picture.
   Ryan used 5 more shapes than Paulo to make his picture.
   How many shapes did Ryan use to make his picture?

   Ryan used _____ shapes to make his picture.

2. Leah bakes 15 muffins.
   Anna bakes 3 fewer muffins than Leah.
   How many muffins does Anna bake?

   Anna bakes _____ muffins.

3.   Maggie read 24 books last month.
She read 7 more books than her brother.
How many books did her brother read last month?

Her brother read _____ books last month.

4.   Brad caught 27 spiders.
Alexis caught 9 more spiders than Brad.
How many spiders did Alexis catch?

Alexis caught _____ spiders.

5.   Jennifer buys 21 stamps from the post office.
Susan buys 14 more stamps than Jennifer.
How many stamps does Susan buy?

Susan buys _____ stamps.

6.   Mr. Rogers had 28 caps in his shop.
He sold 15 of them.
How many caps did Mr. Rogers have left?

Mr. Rogers had _____ caps left.

7. Ling makes 19 friendship bracelets.
She makes 11 fewer friendship bracelets than Karen.
How many friendship bracelets does Karen make?

Karen makes _____ friendship bracelets.

8. Tim has 33 pencils.
Alan has 18 fewer pencils than Tim.
How many pencils does Alan have?

Alan has _____ pencils.

9.   In a big box, there are 4 green toy cars and a small box. Jack opens the small box and there are 6 red toy cars and 7 yellow toy cars.

      a.   How many toy cars are there in the small box?

      b.   How many toy cars are there in all?

_____ + _____ = _____

_____ + _____ = _____

There are _____ toy cars in the big box in all.

10. In January, 3 girls and 5 boys celebrate their birthdays. In February, 7 boys and girls celebrate their birthdays. How many children celebrate their birthdays in January and February?

_____ + _____ = _____

_____ + _____ = _____

_____ children celebrate their birthdays in January and February.

CHAPTER 14 Mental Math Strategies

Worksheet 1   Mental Addition

Complete each number bond.

1.
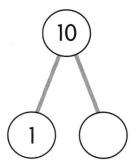

2.
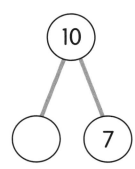

3.
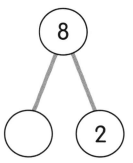

4.
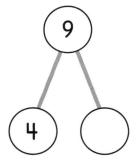

Complete the fact family.

5.
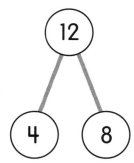

$4 + 8 =$ _____

_____ $+$ _____ $=$ _____

_____ $-$ _____ $=$ _____

_____ $-$ _____ $=$ _____

Make ten.
Then add.

6. 7 + 9 = _____ + _____

= _____

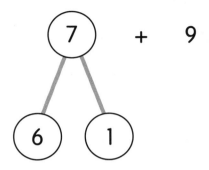

7. 8 + 5 = _____ + _____

= _____

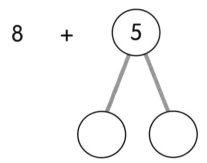

Add.
Use doubles fact.

8. 3 + 3 = _____   **9.** 7 + 7 = _____

Add.
Use doubles facts.

10. 4 + 5 = 4 + _____ + _____

= _____ + 1

= _____

11.   8 + 7 = _____ + _____ + 7

　　　　　= 1 + _____

　　　　　= _____

Add mentally.
First add the ones.
Then add the ones to the tens.

> **Example**
>
> Find 13 + 4.
>
> _____3_____ + 4 = _____7_____
>
> 10 + _____7_____ = _____17_____
>
> So, 13 + 4 = _____17_____.
>
>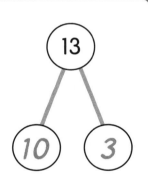

12.   Find 11 + 8.

　　　　_____ + 8 = _____

　　　　10 + _____ = _____

　　　　So, 11 + 8 = _____.

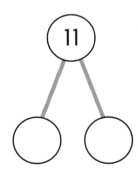

13. Find 24 + 5.

_____ + 5 = _____

_____ + _____ = _____

So, 24 + 5 = _____.

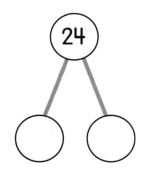

14. Find 32 + 6.

_____ + 6 = _____

_____ + _____ = _____

So, 32 + 6 = _____.

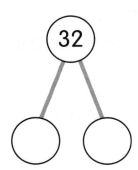

15. 12 + 5 = _____

16. 15 + 3 = _____

17. 23 + 6 = _____

18. 21 + 7 = _____

19. 31 + 4 = _____

20. 8 + 30 = _____

Add mentally.
First add the tens.
Then add the tens to the ones.

> **Example**
>
> Find 16 + 10.
>
> ___10___ + 10 = ___20___
>
> 6 + ___20___ = ___26___
>
> So, 16 + 10 = ___26___.
>
>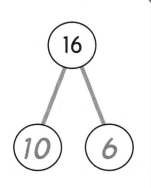

21. Find 14 + 10.

_____ + 10 = _____

4 + _____ = _____

So, 14 + 10 = _____.

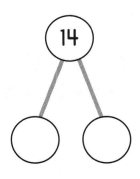

22. Find 27 + 10.

_____ + 10 = _____

_____ + _____ = _____

So, 27 + 10 = _____.

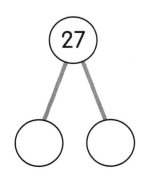

23. Find 20 + 15.

_____ + 10 = _____

_____ + _____ = _____

So, 20 + 15 = _____.

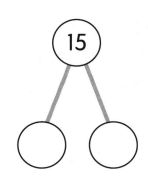

24. 19 + 10 = _____

25. 10 + 11 = _____

26. 10 + 28 = _____

27. 10 + 22 = _____

28. 17 + 20 = _____

29. 20 + 13 = _____

Add mentally.
Use doubles facts.

> **Example**
>
> Find 2 + 3.
>
> 2 + 3 = 2 + __*2*__ + __*1*__
>
> = __*4*__ + __*1*__
>
> = __*5*__

2 + 3 is double 2 plus 1.
2 + 2 is a **doubles fact**.

30. Find 5 + 6.

5 + 6 = 5 + _____ + _____

= _____ + _____

= _____

31. Find 3 + 4.

3 + 4 = 3 + _____ + _____

= _____ + _____

= _____

32. 8 + 9 = _____   **33.** 7 + 6 = _____

Solve mentally.
Fill in the blanks.

34.

I had 23 toy cars.
I just bought 4 more.

Xavier

How many toy cars does Xavier have
in all?

_____

35.

I have 14 hair clips.

I have 10 more hair clips than Isabel.

Isabel   Linda

How many hairclips does Linda have?   _____

Worksheet 2   Mental Subtraction

Subtract mentally.
Think of addition.

Example

Find 8 – 2.

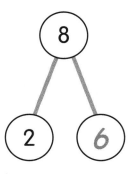

Think of addition.
2 and 6 make 8.

So, 8 – 2 = ___*6*___.

1.   Find 7 – 3.

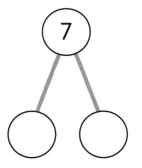

So, 7 – 3 = _____.

2.   Find 13 – 5.

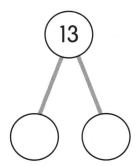

So, 13 – 5 = _____.

3.   9 – 6 = _____

4.   16 – 7 = _____

5.   10 – 6 = _____

6.   17 – 8 = _____

Subtract mentally.
First subtract the ones.
Then add the ones to the tens.

Example

Find 29 − 8.

_____9_____ − 8 = _____1_____

20 + _____1_____ = _____21_____

So, 29 − 8 = _____21_____.

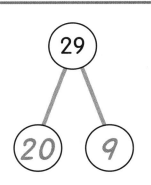

---

7. Find 25 − 2.

_____ − 2 = _____

20 + _____ = _____

So, 25 − 2 = _____.

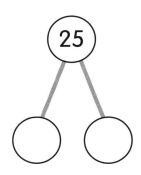

8. Find 34 − 3.

_____ − 3 = _____

30 + _____ = _____

So, 34 − 3 = _____.

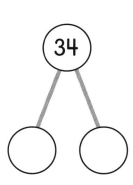

9. 26 − 5 = _____   **10.** 28 − 4 = _____

11. 39 − 9 = _____   **12.** 36 − 4 = _____

Subtract mentally.
First subtract the tens.
Then add the tens to the ones.

Example

Find 24 – 10.

20 – ___10___ = ___10___

4 + ___10___ = ___14___

So, 24 – 10 = ___14___.

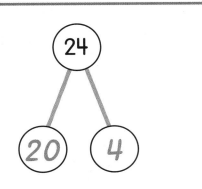

---

13. Find 27 – 10.

20 – _____ = _____

7 + _____ = _____

So, 27 – 10 = _____.

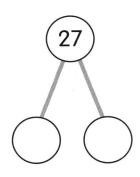

14. Find 35 – 20.

30 – _____ = _____

5 + _____ = _____

So, 35 – 20 = _____.

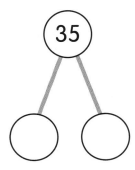

15. 29 – 10 = _____

16. 22 – 20 = _____

17. 34 – 20 = _____

18. 39 – 30 = _____

Solve mentally.
Fill in the blanks.

19.

I have 15 chickens
and 7 ducks.

Farmer John

How many more chickens than ducks
does Farmer John have?   _____

20.

I have 36 marbles.
I give 10 of them away.

Miguel

How many marbles does Miguel have left?   _____

CHAPTER 15 Calendar and Time

Worksheet 1   Using a Calendar

Match the children with their correct position in the line.

1.

Emily | Carlos | Ken | Rick | Fatima |
Gavin | Tiffany | Wilma | Devina | Tom

Wilma	•	• 8th •	• tenth
Devina	•	• 2nd •	• eighth
Gavin	•	• 7th •	• first
Rick	•	• 10th •	• fourth
Emily	•	• 6th •	• seventh
Tom	•	• 1st •	• second
Tiffany	•	• 4th •	• sixth

Name: _____ **Date:** _____

Fill in the blanks.
Use the calendar to help you.

January						
Su	Mo	Tu	We	Th	Fr	Sa
				1	2	3
4	5	6	7	8	9	10
11	12	13	14	15	16	17
18	19	20	21	22	23	24
25	26	27	28	29	30	31

February						
Su	Mo	Tu	We	Th	Fr	Sa
1	2	3	4	5	6	7
8	9	10	11	12	13	14
15	16	17	18	19	20	21
22	23	24	25	26	27	28

March						
Su	Mo	Tu	We	Th	Fr	Sa
1	2	3	4	5	6	7
8	9	10	11	12	13	14
15	16	17	18	19	20	21
22	23	24	25	26	27	28
29	30	31				

April						
Su	Mo	Tu	We	Th	Fr	Sa
			1	2	3	4
5	6	7	8	9	10	11
12	13	14	15	16	17	18
19	20	21	22	23	24	25
26	27	28	29	30		

May						
Su	Mo	Tu	We	Th	Fr	Sa
					1	2
3	4	5	6	7	8	9
10	11	12	13	14	15	16
17	18	19	20	21	22	23
24	25	26	27	28	29	30
31						

June						
Su	Mo	Tu	We	Th	Fr	Sa
	1	2	3	4	5	6
7	8	9	10	11	12	13
14	15	16	17	18	19	20
21	22	23	24	25	26	27
28	29	30				

July						
Su	Mo	Tu	We	Th	Fr	Sa
			1	2	3	4
5	6	7	8	9	10	11
12	13	14	15	16	17	18
19	20	21	22	23	24	25
26	27	28	29	30	31	

August						
Su	Mo	Tu	We	Th	Fr	Sa
						1
2	3	4	5	6	7	8
9	10	11	12	13	14	15
16	17	18	19	20	21	22
23	24	25	26	27	28	29
30	31					

September						
Su	Mo	Tu	We	Th	Fr	Sa
		1	2	3	4	5
6	7	8	9	10	11	12
13	14	15	16	17	18	19
20	21	22	23	24	25	26
27	28	29	30			

October						
Su	Mo	Tu	We	Th	Fr	Sa
				1	2	3
4	5	6	7	8	9	10
11	12	13	14	15	16	17
18	19	20	21	22	23	24
25	26	27	28	29	30	31

November						
Su	Mo	Tu	We	Th	Fr	Sa
1	2	3	4	5	6	7
8	9	10	11	12	13	14
15	16	17	18	19	20	21
22	23	24	25	26	27	28
29	30					

December						
Su	Mo	Tu	We	Th	Fr	Sa
		1	2	3	4	5
6	7	8	9	10	11	12
13	14	15	16	17	18	19
20	21	22	23	24	25	26
27	28	29	30	31		

> A **calendar** shows the **days**, **weeks**, and **months** of a **year**.

2. There are _____ days in one week.

3. The first day of the week is _____.

4. _____ is the day between Wednesday and Friday.

5. The day that comes after August 2 is a _____.

6. The day that comes 1 week before February 19 is a _____.

7. There are _____ months in one year.

8. _____ is the fourth month of the year.

9. October is the _____ month of the year.

10. _____ is the month between July and September.

11. In this calendar, February has _____ days.

12. _____ months of the year have 30 days.

13. In this calendar, Veterans Day (November 11) is on a _____.

Identify the dates.
Follow the directions.
Mark the calendar on the next page.

--- Example ---

Circle the date January 24, 2015 in gray.

2015

January						
Sunday	Monday	Tuesday	Wednesday	Thursday	Friday	Saturday
				1	2	3
4	5	6	7	8	9	10
11	12	13	14	15	16	17
18	19	20	21	22	23	(24)
25	26	27	28	29	30	31

A calendar also helps us to mark a particular **date**.

14. Circle the date January 13, 2015 in red.

15. Mark the date January 29, 2015 with a blue X.

16. Circle the date January 7, 2015 in green.

17. Circle the second Friday of the month in blue.

18.   Mark the last Monday of the month with a red X.

19.   Circle the date 2 days before January 6 in black.

20.   Mark the date 1 week after January 14 with a green X.

2015

January						
Sunday	Monday	Tuesday	Wednesday	Thursday	Friday	Saturday
				1	2	3
4	5	6	7	8	9	10
11	12	13	14	15	16	17
18	19	20	21	22	23	24
25	26	27	28	29	30	31

Look at the pictures.
Fill in each box with the correct season.

> summer   winter   fall   spring

21.

_____

22.

_____

Months help us to know the **seasons** of the year. Some months are **warm**. Some are **cold**.

23.

_____

24.

_____

Fill in the blanks.
Think about the seasons.
In what seasons are these months?

25. July _____

26. October _____

27. May _____

28. December _____

Worksheet 2 Telling Time to the Hour

Write the time.

Example

minute hand

hour hand

When the minute hand is at 12, we read the time as **o'clock**.

We tell time to the **hour** when we use o'clock.

3 o'clock

1.

_____

2.

_____

3.

_____

4.

_____

Name: _____ **Date:** _____

Write the time.

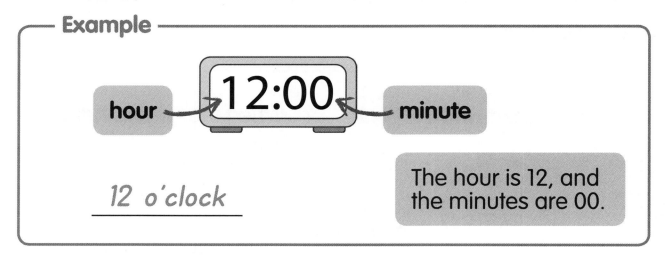

Example

hour → **12:00** ← minute

12 o'clock

The hour is 12, and the minutes are 00.

5. 2:00

_____

6. 9:00

_____

7. 11:00

_____

8. 3:00

_____

9. 7:00

_____

10. 1:00

_____

Match the clock to the correct time.

11.

    •

    •   [1 o'clock]

7:00   •

    •   [9 o'clock]

    •

    •   [7 o'clock]

4:00   •

    •   [12 o'clock]

    •

    •   [4 o'clock]

Write the time.

12.  8:00 _____

13.  5:00 _____

14.  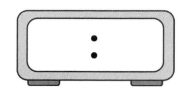 _____

15 .  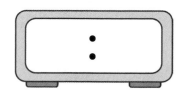 _____

Look at the pictures.
Then fill in the blanks with the correct time.
This is what Desiree does on Tuesday.

> **Example**
>
> Her math class starts at
> _10 o'clock_ .

16.

She finishes school at

_____.

17 .

She does her homework at

_____.

Match the picture to the time.
Circle the correct clock.

18.

  2:00

Natalie goes for a jog in the morning.

19.

  4:00

Mr. Andrews plays golf with his friends in the afternoon.

Worksheet 3   Telling Time to the Half Hour

Write the time.

Example

When the minute hand is at 6, we say it is **half past** the hour.

half past 10

We tell time to the **half hour** when we use half past.

1.

_____

2.

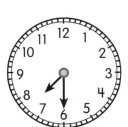

_____

3.

_____

4.

_____

Write the time.

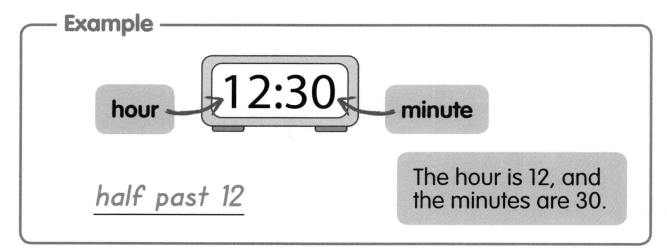

Example

hour ➤ 12:30 ➤ minute

half past 12

The hour is 12, and the minutes are 30.

5. 3:30

_____

6. 7:30

_____

7. 11:30

_____

8. 9:30

_____

9. 5:30

_____

10. 2:30

_____

Match the clock to the correct time.

11.

 •

• half past 11

2:30 •

• half past 8

 •

• half past 5

11:30 •

• half past 6

 •

• half past 2

Write the time.

12.  4:30 _____

13.  6:30 _____

14.  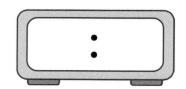 _____

15 .  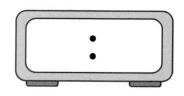 _____

Look at the pictures.
Then fill in the blanks with the correct time.
Marcus goes to the fair with his father.

16.

Marcus and his father reach the fair at _____.

17.

At _____, Marcus and his father take a ride on the roller coaster.

18.

They buy a hotdog from the hotdog stand at _____.

Match the picture to the time.
Circle the correct clock.

19.

8:30

Mrs. Carlos goes to the supermarket in the morning.

20.

5:30

Samuel reads a storybook at night before bedtime.

CHAPTER 16 Numbers to 120

Worksheet 1 Counting to 120

Count in tens.
Fill in the blanks.

Example

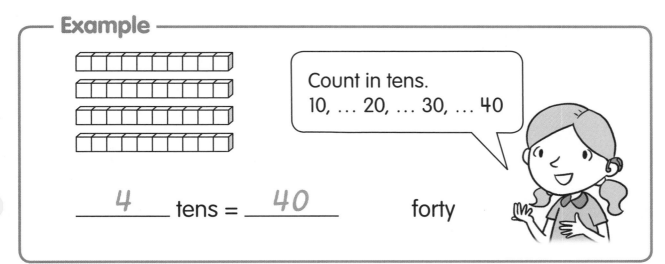

Count in tens.
10, … 20, … 30, … 40

_____4_____ tens = _____40_____ forty

1.

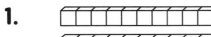
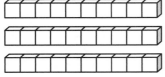
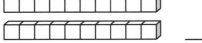

_____ tens = _____ fifty

2.

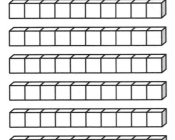

_____ tens = _____ sixty

3.

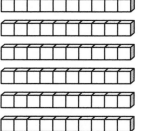

_____ tens = _____   seventy

4.

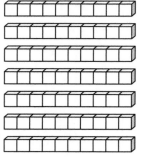

_____ tens = _____   eighty

5.

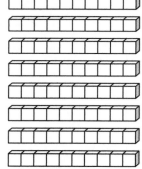

_____ tens = _____   ninety

6.

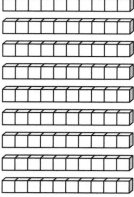

_____ tens = _____   one hundred

Count in tens and ones.
Fill in the blanks.

Example

10, … 20, … 30, … 40, … __*50*__, __*51*__

7.

10, … 20, … 30, … 40, … _____, … _____,

_____, _____, _____

8.

10, … 20, … 30, … 40, … _____, … _____, …

_____, _____, _____, _____, _____,

_____, _____

9.

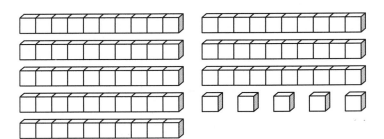

10, … 20, … 30, … 40, … _____, … _____, …

_____, … _____, _____, _____, _____,

_____, _____

10.

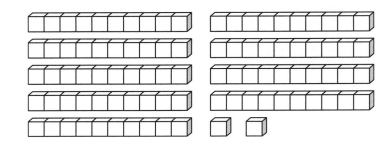

10, … 20, … 30, … 40, … _____, … _____, …

_____, … _____, … _____, _____,

_____

Count.
Write the next number.

11. 99, 100, 101, 102, _____

12. 104, 105, 106, 107, _____

13. 109, 110, 111, 112, 113, 114, _____

14.

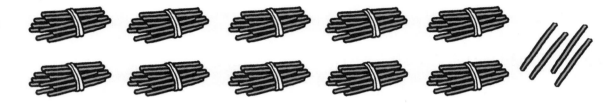

10, … 20, … 30, … 40, … _____, … _____, …

_____, … _____, … _____, … _____, …

_____, _____, _____, _____

15.

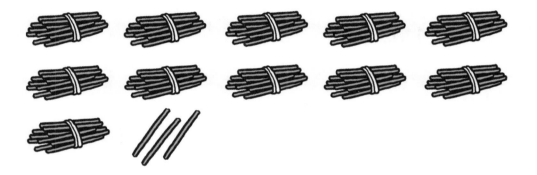

10, … 20, … 30, … 40, … _____, … _____, …

_____, … _____, … _____, … _____, …

_____, _____, _____, _____

Write the number.

16. one hundred sixteen   _____

17. one hundred nine   _____

18. one hundred twenty   _____

19. one hundred twelve   _____

20. one hundred seven   _____

21. one hundred thirteen   _____

Write in words.

22. 103   _____

23. 105   _____

24. 111   _____

25. 119   _____

26. 114   _____

27. 108   _____

Fill in the blanks.

Example

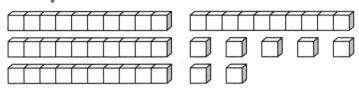

There are 47 ☐.

_____40_____ and _____7_____ make _____47_____.

_____40_____ + _____7_____ = _____47_____

28.

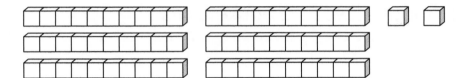

_____ and 2 make 62.

29. 3 and 80 make _____.

30. _____ and 90 make 91.

31. 70 + 8 = _____

32. _____ + 90 = 99

Circle a group of 10.
Then estimate how many basketballs there are.

Example

When you **estimate** the number of an item, you find out about how many there are without counting the actual number.

There are about ___20___ basketballs.

33.

There are about _____ basketballs.

34.

There are about _____ basketballs.

Worksheet 2   Place Value

Look at each picture.
Circle groups of 10.
Then fill in the place-value charts.

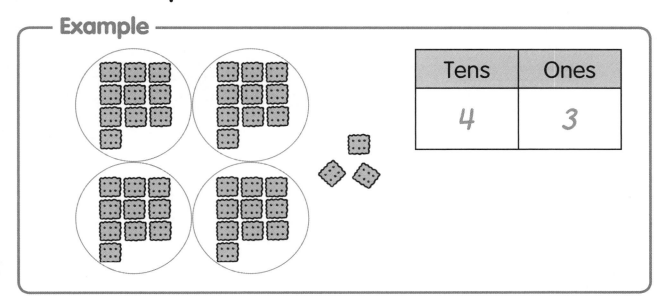

Example

Tens	Ones
4	3

1.

Tens	Ones

2.

Tens	Ones

Name: ______________________ Date: ______________

Fill in the place-value chart on the right.
Then fill in the blanks.

Example

Tens	Ones
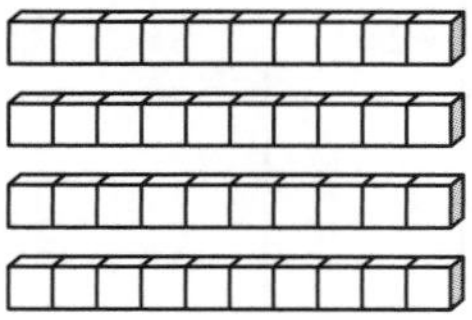	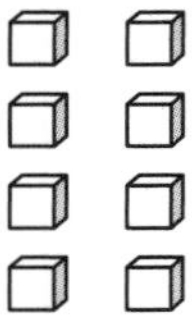

Tens	Ones
4	8

48 = __4__ tens __8__ ones

48 = __40__ + __8__

3.

Tens	Ones
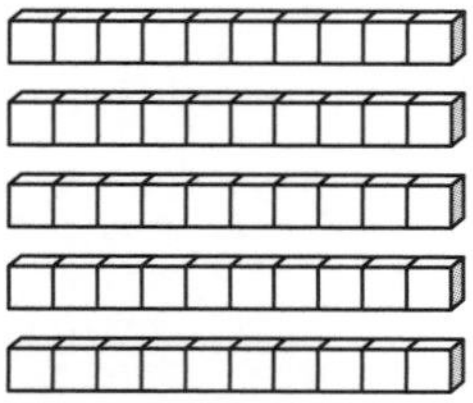	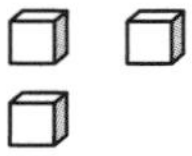

Tens	Ones

53 = ________ tens ________ ones

53 = ________ + ________

4.

Tens	Ones

Tens	Ones

_____ = _____ tens _____ ones

_____ = _____ + _____

5.

Tens	Ones

Tens	Ones

_____ = _____ tens _____ ones

_____ = _____ + _____

Fill in the place-value charts.

6.

Tens	Ones

7.

Tens	Ones

8.

Tens	Ones

Worksheet 3 Comparing, Ordering, and Patterns

Fill in the blanks.
Use the number line to help you.

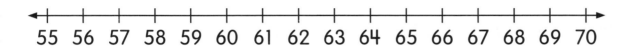

55 56 57 58 59 60 61 62 63 64 65 66 67 68 69 70

> A **number line** can be used to count on, count back, and compare numbers.

Example

2 more than 56 is ___*58*___.

3 less than 70 is ___*67*___.

---

1. 5 less than 70 is _____.

2. 7 more than 55 is _____.

3. _____ is 6 more than 62.

4. _____ is 4 less than 59.

5. 59 is 3 more than _____.

6. 69 is 1 less than _____.

Complete the number line.

7.

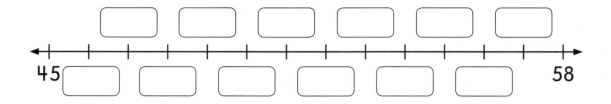

45 ⬚ ⬚ ⬚ ⬚ ⬚ ⬚ 58

Use the number line in Exercise 7 to complete Exercises 8 to 14.

8.   7 less than 57 is _____.

9.   8 more than 48 is _____.

10.   _____ is 10 more than 46.

11.   _____ is 4 less than 52.

12.   _____ is 9 more than 45.

13.   _____ is 5 less than 58.

14.   53 is 7 more than _____.

15.   55 is 1 less than _____.

Compare the numbers.

Example

Which number is greater?
Which number is less?

 48   53

Tens	Ones
4	8

Tens	Ones
5	3

____5____ tens is greater than ____4____ tens.

So, ____53____ is greater than ____48____.

____48____ is less than ____53____.

Compare the tens. The tens
are different.
5 tens is greater than 4 tens.

---

16. Which number is greater?
Which number is less?

 54   70

_____ tens is greater than _____ tens.

So, _____ is greater than _____.

_____ is less than _____.

Compare the numbers.

┌─ **Example** ───

Which number is greater?
Which number is less?

Tens	Ones
4	9

Tens	Ones
4	2

_____9_____ ones is greater than _____2_____ ones.

So, _____49_____ is greater than _____42_____.

_____42_____ is less than _____49_____.

┌───┐
│ Compare the tens. The tens are equal.   │
│ Compare the ones.   │
│ 9 ones is greater than 2 ones.   │
└───┘

└──

17.   Which number is greater?
Which number is less?

_____ ones is greater than _____ ones.

So, _____ is greater than _____.

_____ is less than _____.

Color the greater number.

18.    81   or   50

19.    74   or   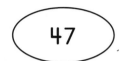 47

20.    69   or   59

21.    45   or   48

Color the number that is less.

22. 53   or   83

23. 64   or   74

24. 65   or   56

25. 90   or   92

Compare the numbers.
Which is the least number?
Which is the greatest number?

┌─ **Example** ───┐

| 85 | 51 | 73 |

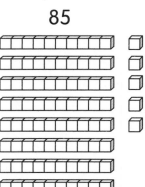

Tens	Ones
8	5

Tens	Ones
5	1

Tens	Ones
7	3

Least: _____*51*_____

Greatest: _____*85*_____

> Compare the tens.
> 5 tens is less than 7 tens and 8 tens.
> 8 tens is more than 5 tens and 7 tens.

└───┘

26.

Tens	Ones
7	8

Tens	Ones
6	2

Tens	Ones
9	1

Least: _____

Greatest: _____

Tens	Ones
7	8
6	2
9	1

Compare the tens.

27.

Tens	Ones
4	5

Tens	Ones
4	9

Tens	Ones
4	3

Least: _____

Greatest: _____

Order the numbers from <u>least</u> to <u>greatest</u>.

28. 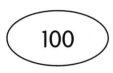      90

_____,   _____,   _____

least   greatest

Order the numbers from <u>greatest</u> to <u>least</u>.

29. 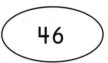      43

_____,   _____,   _____

greatest   least

Complete each number pattern.

30.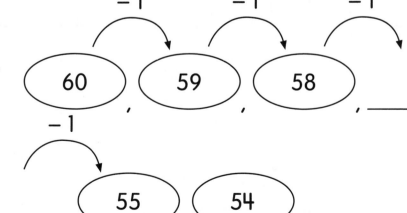

31.

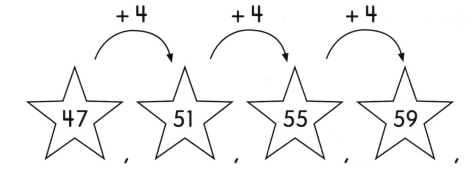

_____ , _____

32.

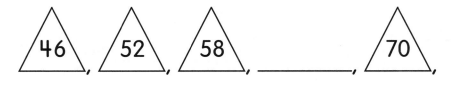

_____ , _____ , 88

33 .

| 83 | , _____ , _____ , | 77 | ,

| 75 | , | 73 |

34.

_____ , _____ , 70 , 67 , 64 , 61

Write the symbol.

35. greater than _____

36. equal _____

37. smaller than _____

Fill in the blank with =, >, or < to make the sentence true.

38. 56 _____ 71

39. 86 _____ 69

40. 77 _____ 77

41. 99 _____ 106

42. 111 _____ 109

43. 120 _____ 88

CHAPTER 17 Addition and Subtraction to 100

Worksheet 1   Addition Without Regrouping

**Complete the number bonds.
Then add.**

1.   24 + 4 = _____

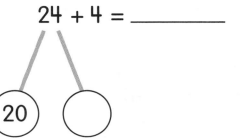

20

Add the ones then add the tens to the ones.

2.   37 + 2 = _____

30

Add using place value.

3.
```
    2    5
+        2
_____
```

4.
```
    3    1
+        4
_____
```

5.
```
    1    4
+   1    2
_____
```

6.
```
    2    3
+   1    5
_____
```

Add by counting on from the greater number.

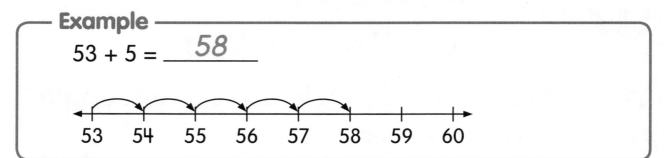

Example

53 + 5 = ___*58*___

7. 60 + 6 = _____

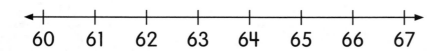

8. 71 + 7 = _____

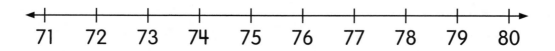

9. 92 + 6 = _____

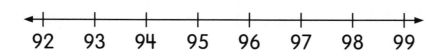

10. 80 + 8 = _____

Complete each place-value chart.
Then add.

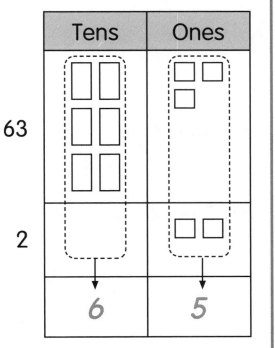

Example

Find 63 + 2.

$$
\begin{array}{cc}
\text{Tens} & \text{Ones} \\
6 & 3 \\
+ \quad\quad & 2 \\
\hline
6 & 5
\end{array}
$$

Step 1 Add the ones.
3 + 2 = 5

Step 2 Add the tens.
60 + 0 = 60

So, 63 + 2 = __65__.

---

11. Find 54 + 3.

$$
\begin{array}{cc}
\text{Tens} & \text{Ones} \\
5 & 4 \\
+ \quad\quad & 3 \\
\hline
\end{array}
$$

Step 1 Add the ones.
4 + 3 = _____

Step 2 Add the tens.
50 + 0 = _____

So, 54 + 3 = _____.

12. Find 71 + 8.

	Tens	Ones
	7	1
+		8
	---	---

	Tens	Ones
71		
8		

Step 1 Add the ones.
1 + 8 = _____

Step 2 Add the tens.
70 + 0 = _____

So, 71 + 8 = _____.

13. Find 42 + 6.

	Tens	Ones
	4	2
+		6
	---	---

	Tens	Ones
42		
6		

Step 1 Add the ones.
_____ + _____ = _____

Step 2 Add the tens.
_____ + _____ = _____

So, 42 + 6 = _____.

Add.

> **Example**
>
> **Step 1** $5 + 2 = $ ___7___
>
> **Step 2** $90 + 0 = $ __90__
>
> So, $95 + 2 = $ __97__.
>
> | Tens | Ones |
> |------|------|
> | 9 | 5 |
> | + | 2 |
> | 9 | 7 |

14. **Step 1** $3 + 5 = $ _____

  Step 2 $70 + 0 = $ _____

  So, $73 + 5 = $ _____.

Tens	Ones
7	3
+	5

15. **Step 1** ____ + ____ = ____

  Step 2 ____ + ____ = ____

  So, $81 + 8 = $ _____.

Tens	Ones
8	1
+	8

16.

Tens	Ones
9	1
+	5

17.

Tens	Ones
8	3
+	4

18.

6	3
+	3

19.

7	7
+	2

Complete each place-value chart.
Then add.

Example

Find 42 + 14.

	Tens	Ones
	4	2
+	1	4
	5	6

	Tens	Ones
42		
14		
	5	6

Step 1 Add the ones.
2 + 4 = 6

Step 2 Add the tens.
40 + 10 = 50

So, 42 + 14 = __56__.

---

20. Find 51 + 26.

	Tens	Ones
	5	1
+	2	6

	Tens	Ones
51		
26		

Step 1 Add the ones.
1 + 6 = _____

Step 2 Add the tens.
50 + 20 = _____

So, 51 + 26 = _____.

21.   Find 65 + 23.

	Tens	Ones

Tens	Ones
6	5
+ 2	3

65

23

Step 1   Add the ones.
5 + 3 = _____

Step 2   Add the tens.
60 + 20 = _____

So, 65 + 23 = _____.

22.   Find 63 + 32.

Tens	Ones

Tens	Ones
6	3
+ 3	2

63

32

Step 1   Add the ones.
_____ + _____ = _____

Step 2   Add the tens.
_____ + _____ = _____

So, 63 + 32 = _____.

Add.

Example

Step 1 $1 + 6 =$ ___7___	
Step 2 $40 + 10 =$ ___50___	
So, $41 + 16 =$ ___57___ .	

Tens	Ones
4	1
+ 1	6
5	7

---

23. **Step 1** $3 + 5 =$ _____

Step 2 $40 + 30 =$ _____

So, $43 + 35 =$ _____ .

Tens	Ones
4	3
+ 3	5

---

24. **Step 1** _____ + _____ = _____

Step 2 _____ + _____ = _____

So, $18 + 41 =$ _____ .

Tens	Ones
1	8
+ 4	1

25.
Tens	Ones
7	8
+ 1	0

26.
Tens	Ones
4	7
+ 1	2

27.
6	3
+ 3	6

28.
5	2
+ 2	4

Worksheet 2 Addition with Regrouping

Regroup the ones into tens and ones.
Then complete the place-value chart.

Example

 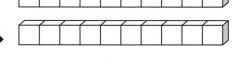

Tens	Ones		Tens	Ones
	26	=	2	6

1.

Tens	Ones		Tens	Ones
	48	=	4	

2.

Tens	Ones		Tens	Ones
	36	=		6

3.

Tens	Ones
	62

=

Tens	Ones
6	

4.

Tens	Ones
	99

=

Tens	Ones

Complete each place-value chart.
Then add.

┌─ **Example** ─────────────────────────────

Find 38 + 4.

```
      Tens      Ones
       1
       3         8
   +             4
   ─────────────────
       4         2
```

Step 1 Add the ones.
8 + 4 = 12

Regroup the ones.
12 ones = 1 ten 2 ones

Step 2 Add the tens.
10 + 30 + 0 = 40

So, 38 + 4 = __42__.

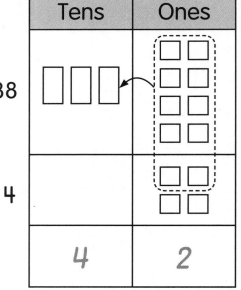

Tens	Ones
38	
4	
4	2

└──

5. Find $49 + 9$.

	Tens	Ones
	4	9
+		9

49

Tens	Ones
□□ □□	□□ □□ □□ □□ □

9

Step 1 Add the ones.

$9 + 9 =$ _____

Regroup the ones.

_____ ones = 1 ten 8 ones

Step 2 Add the tens.

$10 + 40 + 0 =$ _____

So, $49 + 9 =$ _____.

6. Find $58 + 5$.

	Tens	Ones
	5	8
+		5

58

Tens	Ones
	□□ □□ □

5

Step 1 Add the ones.

_____ + _____ = _____

Regroup the ones.

_____ ones = _____ ten _____ ones

Step 2 Add the tens.

_____ + _____ + _____ = _____

So, $58 + 5 =$ _____.

Add.

Example

Step 1 $3 + 8 = \underline{\ 11\ }$

Regroup the ones.
11 ones = 1 ten 1 one

Tens	Ones
5	3
+	8
6	1

Step 2 $10 + 50 + 0 = \underline{\ 60\ }$

So, $53 + 8 = \underline{\ 61\ }$.

---

7. **Step 1** $7 + 5 = \underline{\hspace{1cm}}$

Regroup the ones.
_____ ones = 1 ten 2 ones

Tens	Ones
6	7
+	5

Step 2 $10 + 60 + 0 = \underline{\hspace{1cm}}$

So, $67 + 5 = \underline{\hspace{1cm}}$.

---

8. **Step 1** $\underline{\hspace{1cm}} + \underline{\hspace{1cm}} = \underline{\hspace{1cm}}$

Regroup the ones.
_____ ones = _____ ten
_____ ones

Tens	Ones
4	5
+	5

Step 2 $\underline{\hspace{1cm}} + \underline{\hspace{1cm}} + \underline{\hspace{1cm}} = \underline{\hspace{1cm}}$

So, $45 + 5 = \underline{\hspace{1cm}}$.

9.   5   6
         +   8
         _____

10.   8   7
          +   3
          _____

Complete each place-value chart.
Then add.

┌─ **Example** ───┐

Find 36 + 24.

Tens	Ones
¹	
3	6
+ 2	4

	Tens	Ones
36	□□□	⬚⬚ ⬚⬚ ⬚⬚
24	□□	⬚⬚ ⬚⬚
	6	0

Step 1 Add the ones.
6 + 4 = 10

Regroup the ones.
10 ones = 1 ten 0 ones

Step 2 Add the tens.
10 + 30 + 20 = 60

So, 36 + 24 = _60_.

└──┘

11.   Find 44 + 19.

	Tens	Ones
Tens	4	4
+	1	9

Tens	Ones

44

Step 1   Add the ones.
   4 + 9 = _____

   Regroup the ones.
   _____ ones = 1 ten 3 ones

19

Step 2   Add the tens.
   10 + 40 + 10 = _____

So, 44 + 19 = _____.

12.   Find 58 + 25.

	Tens	Ones
Tens	5	8
+	2	5

Tens	Ones

58

Step 1   Add the ones.
   _____ + _____ = _____

   Regroup the ones.
   _____ ones = _____ ten
               _____ ones

25

Step 2   Add the tens.

   _____ + _____ + _____ = _____

So, 58 + 25 = _____.

Add.

Example

Step 1   3 + 7 = _10_

Regroup the ones.
10 ones = 1 ten 0 one

Step 2   10 + 50 + 10 = _70_

So, 53 + 17 = _70_.

Tens	Ones
$\overset{1}{5}$	3
+ 1	7
7	0

---

13.   **Step 1**   8 + 3 = _____

Regroup the ones.
_____ ones = 1 ten 1 one

Step 2   10 + 50 + 10 = _____

So, 58 + 13 = _____.

Tens	Ones
5	8
+ 1	3

---

14.   **Step 1**   _____ + _____ = _____

Regroup the ones.
_____ ones = _____ ten
_____ ones

Step 2   _____ + _____ + _____ = _____

So, 27 + 65 = _____.

Tens	Ones
2	7
+ 6	5

15.

Tens	Ones
7	2
+ 1	9

16.

Tens	Ones
6	2
+ 2	8

17.

3	9
+ 2	8

18.

2	4
+ 5	8

Worksheet 3   Subtraction Without Regrouping

Complete the number bonds.
Then subtract.

1.   28 – 3 = _____

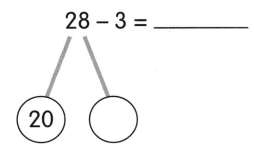

Subtract the ones then add the tens to the ones.

2.   35 – 2 = _____

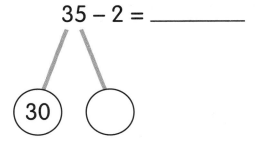

Subtract using place value.

3.   2   5
        –   2
        _____

4.   3   9
        –   4
        _____

5.   2   2
        –   1   0
        _____

6.   3   8
        –   1   3
        _____

Subtract by counting back.

Example

$49 - 7 =$ ____42____

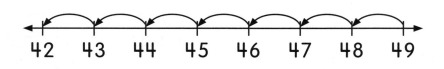

42   43   44   45   46   47   48   49

7. $98 - 5 =$ _____

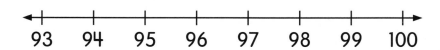

93   94   95   96   97   98   99   100

8. $76 - 4 =$ _____

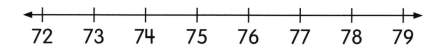

72   73   74   75   76   77   78   79

9. $83 - 3 =$ _____

79   80   81   82   83   84   85   86

10. $67 - 6 =$ _____

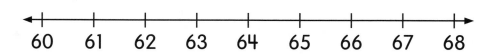

60   61   62   63   64   65   66   67   68

Complete each place-value chart.
Then subtract.

Example

Find 54 – 3.

Tens	Ones
5	4
–	3
5	1

Tens	Ones
54	
5	1

Step 1 Subtract the ones.
4 – 3 = 1

Step 2 Subtract the tens.
50 – 0 = 50

So, 54 – 3 = ___51___.

---

11. Find 48 – 6.

Tens	Ones
4	8
–	6

Tens	Ones
48	

Step 1 Subtract the ones.
8 – 6 = _____

Step 2 Subtract the tens.
40 – 0 = _____

So, 48 – 6 = _____.

12.   Find 44 – 3.

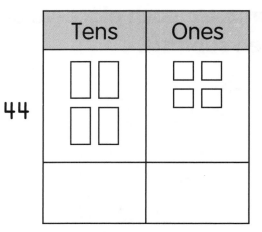

	Tens	Ones

Tens   Ones
  4   4
–_____3_____

Step 1   Subtract the ones.
4 – 3 = _____

Step 2   Subtract the tens.
40 – 0 = _____

So, 44 – 3 = _____.

13.   Find 69 – 2.

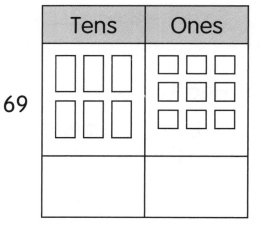

	Tens	Ones

Tens   Ones
  6   9
–_____2_____

Step 1   Subtract the ones.
_____ – _____ = _____

Step 2   Subtract the tens.
_____ – _____ = _____

So, 69 – 2 = _____.

Subtract.

Example

Step 1 5 – 3 = __2__

Step 2 90 – 0 = __90__

So, 95 – 3 = __92__.

Tens	Ones
9	5
–	3
9	2

---

14. **Step 1** 6 – 5 = _____

Step 2 70 – 0 = _____

So, 76 – 5 = _____.

Tens	Ones
7	6
–	5

---

15. **Step 1** _____ – _____ = _____

Step 2 _____ – _____ = _____

So, 57 – 4 = _____.

Tens	Ones
5	7
–	4

16.

Tens	Ones
5	5
–	5

17.

Tens	Ones
8	8
–	6

18.

4	6
–	3

19.

6	9
–	8

Subtract.
Use the place-value chart to help you.

Example

Find 45 – 13.

Tens	Ones
4	5
– 1	3
3	2

Tens	Ones
3	2

45

Step 1 Subtract the ones.
5 – 3 = 2

Step 2 Subtract the tens.
40 – 10 = 30

So, 45 – 13 = _32_.

---

20. Find 59 – 25.

Tens	Ones
5	9
– 2	5

Tens	Ones

59

Step 1 Subtract the ones.
9 – 5 = _____

Step 2 Subtract the tens.
50 – 20 = _____

So, 59 – 25 = _____.

21. Find 68 – 44.

Tens	Ones
6	8
– 4	4

68

Tens	Ones

Step 1 Subtract the ones.
8 – 4 = _____

Step 2 Subtract the tens.
60 – 40 = _____

So, 68 – 44 = _____.

22. Find 77 – 36.

Tens	Ones
7	7
– 3	6

77

Tens	Ones

Step 1 Subtract the ones.
_____ – _____ = _____

Step 2 Subtract the tens.
_____ – _____ = _____

So, 77 – 36 = _____.

Name: _____ **Date:** _____

Subtract.

> **Example**
>
> **Step 1** $7 - 3 =$ __4__ | Tens | Ones |
> | 6 | 7 |
> **Step 2** $60 - 50 =$ __10__ | −5 | 3 |
> | 1 | 4 |
> So, $67 - 53 =$ __14__.

23. **Step 1** $9 - 5 =$ _____

    Step 2 $40 - 30 =$ _____

    So, $49 - 35 =$ _____.

Tens	Ones
4	9
− 3	5

24. **Step 1** _____ − _____ = _____

    Step 2 _____ − _____ = _____

    So, $48 - 13 =$ _____.

Tens	Ones
4	8
− 1	3

25. | Tens | Ones |
    |------|------|
    | 6 | 4 |
    | − 2 | 1 |

26. | Tens | Ones |
    |------|------|
    | 5 | 7 |
    | − 1 | 6 |

27. | 7 | 0 |
    |------|------|
    | − 5 | 0 |

28. | 8 | 4 |
    |------|------|
    | − 3 | 2 |

Worksheet 4   Subtraction with Regrouping

Regroup one ten into ten ones.
Then complete the place-value chart.

Example

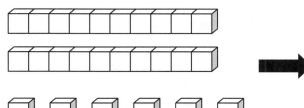

Tens	Ones		Tens	Ones
2	6	=	1	16

1.

Tens	Ones		Tens	Ones
3	4	=	2	

2.

Tens	Ones		Tens	Ones
4	3	=	3	

3.

Tens	Ones
5	7

=

Tens	Ones
	17

Subtract.
Use the place-value chart to help you.

Example

Find 45 – 6.

$$
\begin{array}{cc}
\text{Tens} & \text{Ones} \\
{}^{3}\cancel{4} & {}^{1}5 \\
- & 6 \\
\hline
3 & 9 \\
\end{array}
$$

45

Tens	Ones
3	9

Step 1 Subtract the ones.

Regroup the tens and ones in 45.

45 = 4 tens 5 ones
    = 3 tens 15 ones

15 – 6 = 9

Step 2 Subtract the tens.
30 – 0 = 30

So, 45 – 6 = __39__.

4.   Find 64 − 8.

Tens	Ones

$$\overset{5}{\cancel{6}} \quad \overset{1}{4}$$
$$- 8$$
_____

Step 1   Subtract the ones.

Regroup the tens
and ones in 64.
64 = 6 tens 4 ones
    = 5 tens 14 ones
14 − 8 = _____

Step 2   Subtract the tens.
50 − 0 = _____

So, 64 − 8 = _____.

64

5.   **Step 1**   Subtract the ones.

Regroup the tens and ones
in 82.
8 tens 2 ones = 7 tens
                    _____ ones

_____ − _____ = _____

	Tens	Ones
	8	2
−		5

Step 2   Subtract the tens.

_____ − _____ = _____

So, 82 − 5 = _____.

6. Find 53 – 47.

Tens   Ones

$$\begin{array}{r} {}^{4}\!\!\not5 \quad {}^{1}3 \\ -\ 4 \qquad 7 \\ \hline \end{array}$$

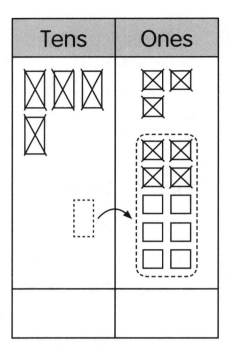

53

Step 1 Subtract the ones.

Regroup the tens
and ones in 53.
53 = 5 tens 3 ones
    = 4 tens 13 ones
13 – 7 = _____

Step 2 Subtract the tens.
40 – 40 = _____

So, 53 – 47 = _____.

7. **Step 1** Subtract the ones.

Regroup the tens and
ones in 76.
7 tens 6 ones = 6 tens

_____ ones

_____ – _____ = _____

Tens   Ones

$$\begin{array}{r} 7 \qquad 6 \\ -\ 3 \qquad 7 \\ \hline \end{array}$$

Step 2 Subtract the tens.

_____ – _____ = _____

So, 76 – 37 = _____.

Name: _____   Date: _____

Regroup and subtract.

Example

Tens	Ones
3	1
4̶	6
−	8
3	8

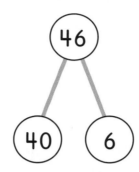 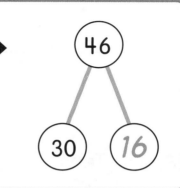

8.

Tens	Ones
5	2
−	6

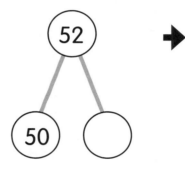 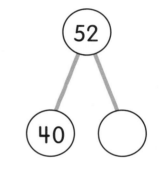

9.

Tens	Ones
6	4
−	7

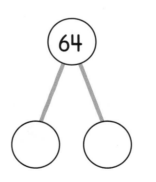 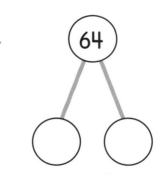

10.

Tens	Ones
9	1
− 3	3

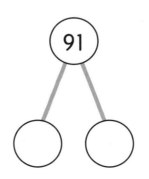 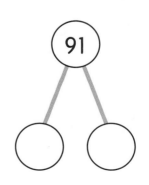

11.

Tens	Ones
³4̶	¹3
− 1	8

12.

Tens	Ones
8	4
−	6

13.

Tens	Ones
⁶7̶	¹4
− 1	9

14.

Tens	Ones
6	2
− 3	7

15.

6	0
−	5

16.

9	7
−	9

17.

5	4
− 4	5

18.

7	3
− 4	4

CHAPTER 18 Getting Ready for Multiplication and Division

Worksheet 1   Adding the Same Number

Add.

1.   3 + 3 = _____

2.   7 + 7 = _____

3.   4 + 4 + 4 = _____

4.   5 + 5 + 5 = _____

5.   8 + 8 = _____

6.   2 + 2 + _____ = 6

Count the number of groups.
Then count the number of items in each group.
Write the numbers in the blanks.

Example

4 + 4 = ___*8*___

2 fours = ___*8*___

4 + 4 means
2 fours or
2 **groups** of 4.

Each group
has the
same
number
of rackets.

7.

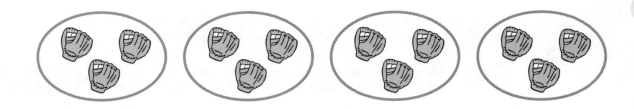

$3 + 3 + 3 + 3 =$ _____

4 threes = _____

8.

$7 + 7 + 7 =$ _____

3 sevens = _____

9.

$6 + 6 + 6 + 6 =$ _____

4 sixes = _____

Match.

10.   9 + 9 + 9 + 9 •   • 5 groups of 5

4 groups of 2 •   • 6 fours

5 fives   •   • 2 + 2 + 2 + 2

8 + 8 + 8   •   • 4 nines

6 groups of 4 •   • 3 eights

Look at the pictures.
Then fill in the blanks.

┌─ **Example** ───────────────────────────────────────┐

_2_ + _2_ + _2_ + _2_ + _2_ = _10_

_5_ twos = _10_

There are _10_ fish in all.
└───────────────────────────────────────┘

11.

_____ + _____ + _____ + _____ = _____

_____ fours = _____

There are _____ tops in all.

12.

_____ + _____ + _____ = _____

_____ fives = _____

There are _____ strawberries in all.

13.

_____ + _____ + _____ + _____ = _____

_____ sevens = _____

There are _____ candles in all.

**Look at the pictures.
Then fill in the blanks.**

Example

There are ___4___ groups.

Each group has ___3___ marbles.

3 + 3 + 3 + 3 = ___12___

4 _threes_ = ___12___

There are ___12___ marbles in all.

14.

There are _____ groups.

Each group has _____ hearts.

5 + 5 + _____ + _____ + _____ + _____ = _____

6 _____ = _____

There are _____ hearts in all.

15.

There are _____ groups.

Each group has _____ watermelons.

4 _____ = _____

There are _____ watermelons in all.

16. Each bracelet has 10 beads.

5 tens = _____

5 bracelets have _____ beads.

17. Each basket has _____ eggs.

7 _____ = _____

7 baskets have _____ eggs.

Worksheet 2   Sharing Equally

Look at the pictures.
Then fill in the blanks.

Example

There are ____9____ leaves in all.

There are ____3____ groups.

There are ____3____ leaves in each group.

1.

 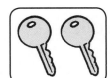  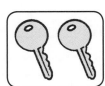

There are _____ keys in all.

There are _____ groups.

There are _____ keys in each group.

2.

There are _____ oranges in all.

There are _____ bags.

There are _____ oranges in each bag.

3.

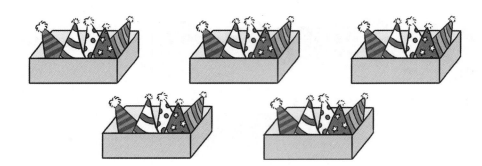

There are _____ party hats in all.

There are _____ boxes.

There are _____ party hats in each box.

4.

There are _____ cherries in all.

There are _____ cakes.

There are _____ cherries on each cake.

5.

There are _____ frogs in all.

There are _____ lily pads.

There are _____ frogs on each lily pad.

Name: _____   Date: _____

Draw.
Then fill in the blanks.

Example

There are 6 ribbons.
Put the 6 ribbons equally into 2 groups.

Put 1 ribbon into each group. Put another ribbon into each group. Do this until you have no ribbons left.

There are ___*3*___ ribbons
in each group.

---

6.   There are 16 smiley faces.
Put the 16 smiley faces equally into 4 groups.

There are _____ smiley faces in each group.

Name: _____   **Date:** _____

7. There are 14 socks.
They are shared equally by 7 children.
How many socks does each child get?

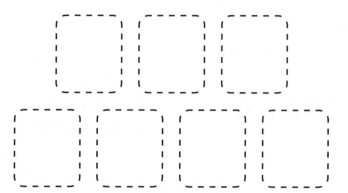 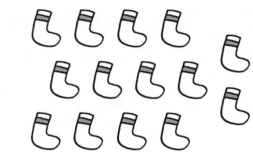

Each child gets _____ socks.

8. There are 20 buttons.
Mrs. Watson sews the buttons onto 4 T-shirts equally.
How many buttons are sewed onto each T-shirt?

_____ buttons are sewed onto each T-shirt.

Share equally.
Then fill in the blank.

Example

Put 10 mangoes into 5 equal groups.

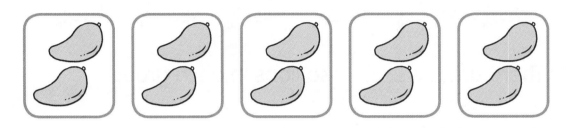

There are _____2_____ mangoes
in each group.

To **share equally**
means to put the
same number
of items into each
group.

9. Put 18 mugs into 3 equal groups.

There are _____ mugs in each group.

10.   Put 12 sea lions into 4 equal groups.

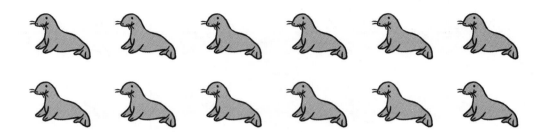

There are _____ sea lions in each group.

11.   Put 28 pencils into 7 equal groups.

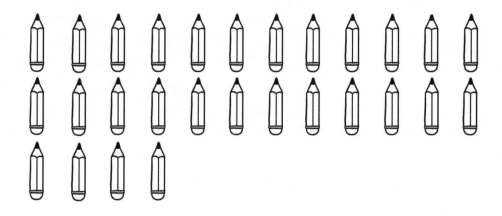

There are _____ pencils in each group.

12.   Put 20 feathers into 2 equal groups.

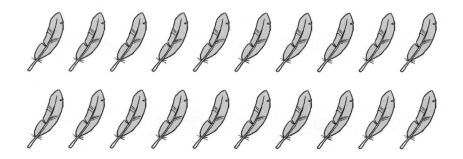

There are _____ feathers in each group.

Worksheet 3   Finding the Number of Groups

Circle.
Then fill in the blanks.

> ## Example
>
> There are 6 hats.
> Circle groups of 2.
>
>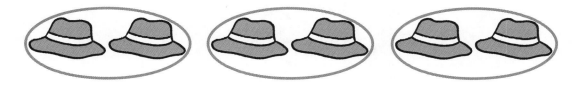
>
> There are _____*3*_____ groups of 2 hats.

1.   There are 18 snails.
     Circle groups of 3.

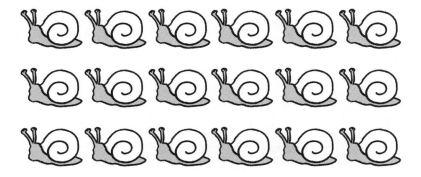

There are _____ groups of 3 snails.

2. There are 25 cabbages.
Circle groups of 5.

There are _____ groups of 5 cabbages.

3. There are 21 erasers.
Circle groups of 7.

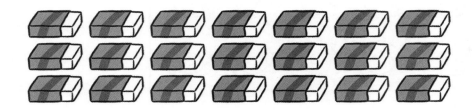

There are _____ groups of 7 erasers.

Solve.

4. A farmer has 12 chickens on his farm.
He puts 3 chickens in each coop.
How many coops are there?

There are _____ coops.

5. Mrs. Walker buys 32 roses.
She puts 4 roses into each vase.
How many vases does Mrs. Walker need?

Mrs. Walker needs _____ vases.

6. Anna brought 27 bookmarks to school.
She gave 3 bookmarks to each of her close friends.
How many close friends does Anna have?

Anna has _____ close friends.

7. Ethan collects stickers.
He has 30 stickers.
He puts 5 stickers on each page of his sticker album.
How many pages does Ethan need?

Ethan needs _____ pages.

CHAPTER 19 Money

Worksheet 1   Penny, Nickel, and Dime

Name each coin.

1.   _____

2.   _____

3.   _____

4.   _____

Count the pennies to find the price of each item.

5.   _____

6.

   _____

7.

     _____

Fill in the blanks using these words.

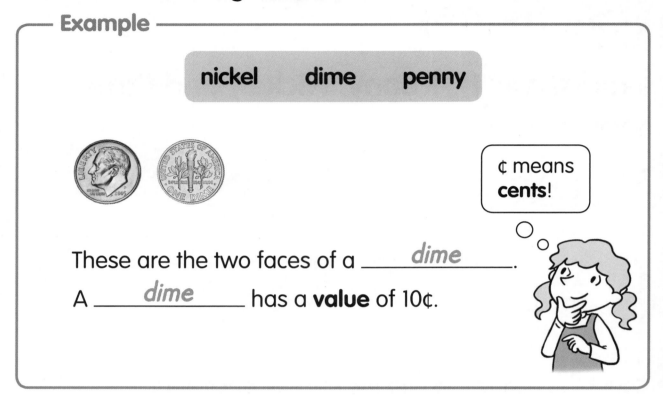

— Example —

| nickel | dime | penny |

¢ means **cents**!

These are the two faces of a ____dime____.

A ____dime____ has a **value** of 10¢.

8.

These are the two faces of a _____.

A _____ has a value of 1¢.

9.

These are the two faces of a _____.

A _____ has a value of 5¢.

Find the value of the group of coins.

Example

_____14_____ ¢

Skip-count by 5s. Then count on in 1s.

10.

_____ ¢

11.

_____ ¢

Skip-count by 5s for nickels. Skip-count by 10s for dimes.

Name: _____   **Date:** _____

12.

_____ ¢

13.

_____ ¢

14.

_____ ¢

Count on from the coin with the greatest value.

Exchange the given coins for a set of coins of equal value.

Draw pennies as , nickels as , and dimes as .

Example

1 nickel

1 nickel = 5¢
1 penny = 1¢
So, 1 nickel = 5 pennies.

Exchange 1 nickel for ___5___ pennies.

---

15. 1 dime

Exchange 1 dime for _____ pennies.

16. 1 dime

Exchange 1 dime for _____ nickels.

17. 1 dime

Exchange 1 dime for _____ nickel and _____ pennies.

Complete the table.

Coins	Items	Draw coins to show the same value in another way
Example	6¢	5¢ 1¢
18.	15¢	
19.	22¢	

Worksheet 2 Quarter

Fill in the blank.

1.

These are the two faces of a **quarter**.

A quarter has a value of _____¢.

Fill in the blanks.

2.   1 can be exchanged for _____ pennies.

3.  1 can be exchanged for _____ nickels.

4.   1 can be exchanged for _____ nickels.

Use pennies (1¢), nickels (5¢), dimes (10¢), and quarters (25¢) to pay for the bracelet.

25¢

┌─ **Example** ──────────────────────────────────┐

  1 coin: (**25¢**)

└──┘

5.   3 coins: (**10¢**) (**10¢**)

6.   4 coins: (**10¢**)

7.   5 coins:

8.   8 coins:

Worksheet 3   Counting Money

Count on to find the value.

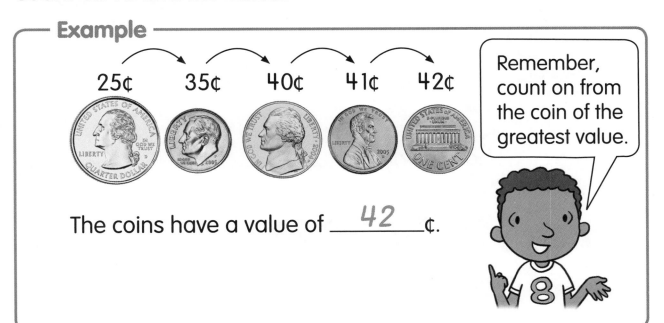

— **Example** —

25¢   35¢   40¢   41¢   42¢

Remember, count on from the coin of the greatest value.

The coins have a value of ___42___ ¢.

1.

The coins have a value of _____¢.

2.

The coins have a value of _____¢.

3.

The coins have a value of _____¢.

4.

The coins have a value of _____¢.

Circle the coins you need to buy each item.

Example

Notepad 55¢

5.

6.

7.

Complete the table.

Coins	Value	Draw coins to show the value in another way
Example	65¢	25¢ 10¢ 10¢ 10¢ 5¢ 5¢
8.	52¢	
9.	_____	

Worksheet 4   Adding and Subtracting Money

Add.

Example

20¢   5¢

20¢ + 5¢ = _____25¢_____

1.

50¢   50¢

50¢ + 50¢ = _____

2.

12¢

12¢ + _____ = _____

3.

_____ + _____ = _____

4.

_____ + _____ = _____

5. 35¢ +

_____ + _____ = _____

6. 48¢ +

_____ + _____ = _____

These are some of the things sold at the school bookstore.
Solve.

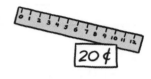

--- **Example** ---

Sonia buys  and  .

___25¢___ + ___15¢___ = ___40¢___

She spends ___40¢___.

7. Zachary buys and  .

_____ + _____ = _____

He spends _____.

8. Jenny buys   and  .

_____ + _____ + _____ = _____

She spends _____.

Subtract.

┌─ **Example** ──┐

    20¢ from 50¢

    50¢ − ___*20¢*___ = ___*30¢*___

└──┘

9.   15¢ from 40¢

    40¢ − _____ = _____

10.   36¢ from 48¢

    _____ − _____ = _____

11.   27¢ from 59¢

    _____ − _____ = _____

12.   12¢ from 3 quarters

    _____ − _____ = _____

13.   53¢ from 4 dimes and 7 nickels

    _____ − _____ = _____

Subtract.

┌─ **Example** ──┐

8¢ from

┌──────────────────┐
│ 1 dime = 10¢   │
│ 2 dimes = 20¢   │
└──────────────────┘

_20¢_ – _8¢_ = _12¢_

└───┘

14. 30¢ from

_____ – _____ = _____

15. 19¢ from

_____ – _____ = _____

16. 42¢ from

_____ – _____ = _____

17. 55¢ from

_____ – _____ = _____

Name: _____   Date: _____

Find the change.

Example

You pay with 20¢ for .

Change = __20¢__ – __15¢__

= __5¢__

---

18. You pay with 38¢ for .

Change = _____ – _____

= _____

19. You pay with 70¢ for .

Change = _____ – _____

= _____

20. You pay with 2 quarters and 3 nickels for .

Change = _____ – _____

= _____

21. You pay with 4 quarters for .

Change = _____ – _____

= _____

Solve.

┌─ **Example** ───┐

Rachel buys a pencil and a sharpener.
How much does she spend in all?

$15¢ + 45¢ = 60¢$

She spends ___*60¢*___ in all.

└──┘

22. Luke has 82¢.
He buys a toy bicycle.
How much money does Luke have left?

Luke has _____ left.

23. After buying a packet of stickers, Kelly has 11¢ left.
How much money did she have at first?

She had _____ at first.

24. Sam buys a pen.
Brad buys a ball.
How much less does Sam pay than Brad?

Sam pays _____ less than Brad.

25. Sucre's mother gives him four nickels and three quarters.
How much money does Sucre have in all?

Sucre has _____ in all.

26. Janice buys a stapler for 27¢.
She gives the cashier two dimes and two nickels.
How much change does Janice get?

Janice gets _____ in change.

Answers

Chapter 10

Worksheet 1

1.

2.

3. greater   4. less
5. shortest   6. longest
7. heavier; lighter   8. as heavy as
9. lighter; heavier   10. as heavy as
11. dog   12. cat
13. dog   14. cat
15. mouse   16. mouse
17. key   18. box of crayons
19. key   20. box of crayons
21. pair of shoes   22. pair of shoes

Worksheet 2

1. 5   2. 14
3. 20   4. 9
5. 17   6. 7
7. 5   8. 12
9. 15   10. orange; apple
11. 9   12. 6
13. glue; notepad   14. 5
15. 8   16. 12
17. kettle   18. toaster
19. kettle   20. kettle
21. cooker

Worksheet 3

1. 3   2. 7
3. 6   4. 12
5. 10   6. 18
7. 6   8. 10

9. shampoo   10. soap
11. soap   12. shampoo
13. 7   14. 12
15. 4   16. C
17. B
18. <u>Box B</u>, <u>Box A</u>, <u>Box C</u>
    heaviest   lightest

Chapter 11

Worksheet 1

1. 4   2. 2
3. 7   4. 12
5. There are <u>2</u> carrots.
   There are <u>5</u> eggs.
   There are more <u>eggs</u> than <u>carrots</u>.
6. There are <u>11</u> shells.
   There are <u>4</u> mushrooms.
   There are more <u>shells</u> than <u>mushrooms</u>.
7. There are <u>7</u> burgers.
   There are <u>9</u> buns.
   There are more <u>buns</u> than <u>burgers</u>.
8. There are <u>3</u> apples.
   There are <u>5</u> oranges.
   There are fewer <u>apples</u> than <u>oranges</u>.
9. There are <u>10</u> notepads.
   There are <u>8</u> envelopes.
   There are fewer <u>envelopes</u> than <u>notepads</u>.
10. There are <u>4</u> rabbits.
    There are <u>6</u> cats.
    There are fewer <u>rabbits</u> than <u>cats</u>.
11. 10   12. 4
13. 6   14. elephants
15. zebras   16. zebras
17. elephants   18. 7
19. 5   20. 3
21. apples   22. oranges
23. apples   24. oranges
25. 15

Worksheet 2

1. 6   2. 8
3. 5   4. blue
5. 3   6. blue
7. 19   8. 7
9. 8   10. 7
11. birds/kittens   12. 4

13. puppies 14. birds; kittens
15. Grace: 5; Angie: 4; Carlos: 6
    Kevin: 1; Dennis: 2
16. Kevin 17. Carlos
18. Kevin 19. 18

Worksheet 3

1.

Fruit	Tally	Number
Cherry	ⵜⵜⵜ ///	8
Strawberry	ⵜⵜⵜ ⵜⵜⵜ ⵜⵜⵜ	15
Banana	ⵜⵜⵜ /	6

2.

Shape	Tally	Number
Rectangle	ⵜⵜⵜ	5
Circle	ⵜⵜⵜ ⵜⵜⵜ ////	14
Triangle	///	3

3.

School Supplies	Tally	Number
Book	ⵜⵜⵜ	5
File	ⵜⵜⵜ //	7
Pencil	////	4

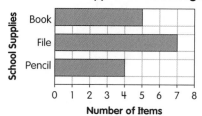

School Supplies Emelda Bought

4.

Flower	Tally	Number
Rose	//	2
Lily	ⵜⵜⵜ /	6
Daisy	ⵜⵜⵜ	5

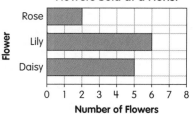

Flowers Sold at a Florist

5.

Toy	Tally	Number
Toy boat	ⵜⵜⵜ ⵜⵜⵜ /	11
Toy car	ⵜⵜⵜ	5
Building blocks	ⵜⵜⵜ ///	8

6.

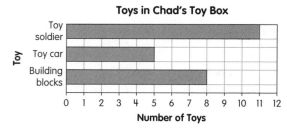

Toys in Chad's Toy Box

7. toy soldiers 8. toy cars
9. 16

10.

Fruit Juice	Tally	Number
Orange	ⵜⵜⵜ ⵜⵜⵜ	10
Cranberry	////	4
Grape	ⵜⵜⵜ //	7
Apple	////	4

11.

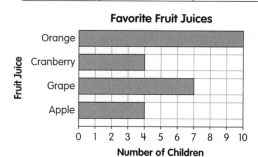

Favorite Fruit Juices

12. cranberry; apple
13. 3

Chapter 12

Worksheet 1

1.

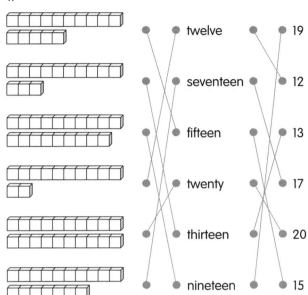

2. 14 is <u>10</u> and <u>4</u>.
   10 and 4 make <u>14</u>.
   10 + <u>4</u> = 14

3. 17 is <u>10</u> and <u>7</u>.
   10 and 7 make <u>17</u>.
   10 + <u>7</u> = 17

4. 10, … 20, 21, 22, 23, 24, 25, 26, 27, 28, 29
   There are <u>29</u> ▱.

5. 10, … 20, … 30, … 40
   There are <u>40</u> ▱.

6. 27   7. 31   8. 39
9. 24   10. 30   11. 21
12. 28   13. 33   14. 37
15. 35   16. 29   17. 40
18. 31

19.
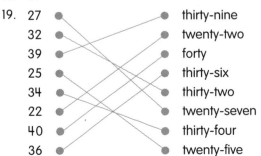

27	thirty-nine
32	twenty-two
39	forty
25	thirty-six
34	thirty-two
22	twenty-seven
40	thirty-four
36	twenty-five

20. There are <u>25</u> ▱.
    Twenty and <u>five</u> make twenty-five.
    <u>20</u> + 5 = <u>25</u>

21. There are <u>34</u> ▱.
    Thirty and <u>four</u> make thirty-four.
    <u>30</u> + 4 = <u>34</u>

Worksheet 2

1. 11 is <u>1</u> ten <u>1</u> one.
   11 = <u>10</u> + <u>1</u>

2. 16 is <u>1</u> ten <u>6</u> ones.
   16 = <u>10</u> + <u>6</u>

3.
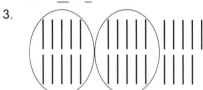

Tens	Ones
2	9

4.
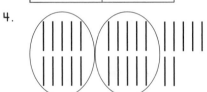

Tens	Ones
2	7

5.
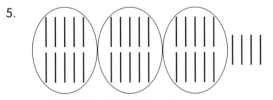

Tens	Ones
3	4

6.

Tens	Ones
4	0

7.

Tens	Ones
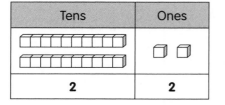	🗆 🗆
2	**2**

22

8.

Tens	Ones
	🗆 🗆
	🗆 🗆
	🗆 🗆
	🗆
3	**7**

37

9. 30 = <u>3</u> tens <u>0</u> ones
   30 + 0 = <u>30</u>

Tens	Ones
3	**0**

10. 33 = <u>3</u> tens <u>3</u> ones
    30 + 3 = <u>33</u>

Tens	Ones
3	**3**

Worksheet 3

1. 19
2. 12
3. 19
4. 12
5. <u>19</u>, <u>15</u>, <u>12</u>
   greatest   least
6. 10, 12, <u>14</u>, 16, <u>18</u>, 20
7. <u>17</u>, 15, <u>13</u>, 11, 9, <u>7</u>
8. 29
9. 38
10. 39
11. 22
12. 29
13. 31

14.

	Tens	Ones
32	**3**	**2**

	Tens	Ones
27	**2**	**7**

<u>32</u> is greater than <u>27</u>.
<u>27</u> is less than <u>32</u>.

15.

	Tens	Ones
23	**2**	**3**

	Tens	Ones
36	**3**	**6**

<u>36</u> is greater than <u>23</u>.
<u>23</u> is less than <u>36</u>.

16.

	Tens	Ones
28	**2**	**8**

	Tens	Ones
21	**2**	**1**

<u>28</u> is greater than <u>21</u>.
<u>21</u> is less than <u>28</u>.

17.

	Tens	Ones
34	**3**	**4**

	Tens	Ones
37	**3**	**7**

<u>37</u> is greater than <u>34</u>.
<u>34</u> is less than <u>37</u>.

18. Set A: 29
    Set B: 22
    Set <u>A</u>
    <u>29</u> is greater than <u>22</u>.
19. Set A: 33
    Set B: 38
    Set <u>B</u>
    <u>38</u> is greater than <u>33</u>.
20. Set A: 21
    Set B: 26
    Set <u>A</u>
    <u>21</u> is less than <u>26</u>.
21. Set A: 40
    Set B: 35
    Set <u>B</u>
    <u>35</u> is less than <u>40</u>.
22. 36
23. 32
24. 27
25. 29
26. <u>36</u> is the greatest number.
    <u>23</u> is the least number.
    <u>23</u>, <u>31</u>, <u>36</u>
    least   greatest
27. <u>35</u> is the greatest number.
    <u>20</u> is the least number.
    <u>35</u>, <u>28</u>, <u>20</u>
    greatest   least
28. <u>40</u> is the greatest number.
    <u>25</u> is the least number.
    <u>40</u>, <u>34</u>, <u>25</u>
    greatest   least
29. 24, <u>25</u>, <u>26</u>, 27, 28, <u>29</u>, 30
30. <u>33</u>, 32, 31, <u>30</u>, <u>29</u>, 28, <u>27</u>
31. 22, 25, <u>28</u>, 31, <u>34</u>, 37, <u>40</u>
32. 34, <u>32</u>, 30, <u>28</u>, 26, 24, <u>22</u>
33. 20, 24, <u>28</u>, 32, <u>36</u>, 40
34. <u>38</u>, <u>34</u>, 30, 26, <u>22</u>, 18

Worksheet 1

1. $9 + 5 = \underline{14}$

   (1) (4)

2. $6 + 7 = \underline{13}$

   (4) (3)

3. $12 + 2 = \underline{14}$

   (10) (2)

4. $15 + 4 = \underline{19}$

   (10) (5)

5. $\underline{3} + \underline{4} = \underline{7}$

6. $\underline{8} + \underline{5} = \underline{13}$

7. $\underline{6} + \underline{9} = \underline{15}$

8. 20, 21, 22, 23, 24, 25
   $20 + 5 = \underline{25}$

9. 31, 32, 33, 34, 35, 36, 37
   $31 + 6 = \underline{37}$

10. 32, 33, 34, 35, 36, 37, 38, 39
    $32 + 7 = \underline{39}$

11.
Tens	Ones
2	1
+	4
2	5

Tens	Ones

    21

    4

    Step 1
    Add the ones.
    $1 + 4 = \underline{5}$
    Step 2
    Add the tens.
    $20 + 0 = \underline{20}$
    So, $21 + 4 = \underline{25}$.

12.
Tens	Ones
2	3
+	3
2	6

    23

    3

    Step 1
    Add the ones.
    $3 + 3 = \underline{6}$
    Step 2
    Add the tens.
    $20 + 0 = \underline{20}$
    So, $23 + 3 = \underline{26}$.

13.
Tens	Ones
3	3
+	5
3	8

    33

    5

    Step 1
    Add the ones.
    $\underline{3} + \underline{5} = \underline{8}$
    Step 2
    Add the tens.
    $\underline{30} + \underline{0} = \underline{30}$
    So, $33 + 5 = \underline{38}$.

14.
Tens	Ones
3	1
+	8
3	9

    31

    8

    Step 1
    Add the ones.
    $1 + \underline{8} = \underline{9}$
    Step 2
    Add the tens.
    $\underline{30} + \underline{0} = \underline{30}$
    So, $31 + 8 = \underline{39}$.

15. **Step 1** $5 + 4 = \underline{9}$
    Step 2 $20 + 0 = \underline{20}$
    So, $25 + 4 = \underline{29}$.

Tens	Ones
2	5
+	4
2	9

16. **Step 1** $\underline{2} + \underline{3} = \underline{5}$
    Step 2 $\underline{30} + \underline{0} = \underline{30}$
    So, $32 + 3 = \underline{35}$.

Tens	Ones
3	2
+	3
3	5

17.
Tens	Ones
2	3
+	2
2	5

18.
Tens	Ones
3	7
+	1
3	8

19.

	Tens	Ones
	1	5
+	2	4
	3	**9**

Step 1
Add the ones.
$5 + 4 = \underline{9}$
Step 2
Add the tens.
$10 + 20 = \underline{30}$
So, $15 + 24 = \underline{39}$.

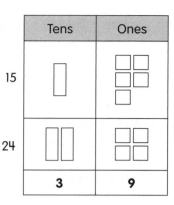

	Tens	Ones
15		
24		
	3	**9**

20.

	Tens	Ones
	1	3
+	2	1
	3	**4**

Step 1
Add the ones.
$3 + 1 = \underline{4}$
Step 2
Add the tens.
$10 + 20 = \underline{30}$
So, $13 + 21 = \underline{34}$.

	Tens	Ones
13		
21		
	3	**4**

21.

	Tens	Ones
	3	0
+	1	0
	4	**0**

Step 1
Add the ones.
$\underline{0} + \underline{0} = \underline{0}$
Step 2
Add the tens.
$\underline{30} + \underline{10} = \underline{40}$
So, $30 + 10 = \underline{40}$.

	Tens	Ones
30		
10		
	4	**0**

22.

	Tens	Ones
	2	0
+	1	7
	3	**7**

Step 1
Add the ones.
$\underline{0} + \underline{7} = \underline{7}$
Step 2
Add the tens.
$\underline{20} + \underline{10} = \underline{30}$
So, $20 + 17 = \underline{37}$.

	Tens	Ones
20		
17		
	3	**7**

23. **Step 1** $9 + 0 = \underline{9}$
Step 2 $10 + 20 = \underline{30}$
So, $19 + 20 = \underline{39}$.

	Tens	Ones
	1	9
+	2	0
	3	**9**

24. **Step 1** $\underline{2} + \underline{4} = \underline{6}$
Step 2 $\underline{20} + \underline{10} = \underline{30}$
So, $22 + 14 = \underline{36}$.

	Tens	Ones
	2	2
+	1	4
	3	**6**

25.

	Tens	Ones
	1	5
+	1	2
	2	**7**

22.

	Tens	Ones
	2	1
+	1	6
	3	**7**

Worksheet 2

1.

Tens	Ones		Tens	Ones
	18	=	**1**	**8**

2.

Tens	Ones		Tens	Ones
	21	=	**2**	**1**

3.

Tens	Ones		Tens	Ones
	25	=	**2**	**5**

4.

	Tens	Ones
	1	9
+		5
	2	**4**

Step 1
Add the ones.
$9 + 5 = \underline{14}$
Regroup the ones.
$\underline{14}$ ones = 1 ten 4 ones
Step 2
Add the tens.
$10 + 10 + 0 = \underline{20}$
So, $19 + 5 = \underline{24}$.

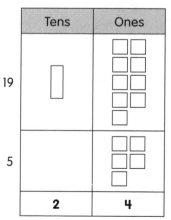

	Tens	Ones
19		
5		
	2	**4**

5.
```
Tens   Ones
  2      6
+        8
  3      4      26
```
Step 1
Add the ones.
6 + 8 = 14
Regroup the ones.   8
14 ones = 1 ten 4 ones
Step 2
Add the tens.
10 + 20 + 0 = 30
So, 26 + 8 = 34.

Tens	Ones
3	4

6. **Step 1** 3 + 7 = 10
   Regroup the ones.
   10 ones = 1 ten 0 ones
   Step 2 10 + 30 + 0 = 40
   So, 33 + 7 = 40.

```
Tens   Ones
  3      3
+        7
  4      0
```

7. **Step 1** 7 + 4 = 11
   Regroup the ones.
   11 ones = 1 ten 1 one
   Step 2 10 + 20 + 0 = 30
   So, 27 + 4 = 31.

```
Tens   Ones
  2      7
+        4
  3      1
```

8.
```
  1   7
+     3
  2   0
```

9.
```
  1   6
+     8
  2   4
```

10.
```
Tens   Ones
  1      2
+ 1      9
  3      1      12
```

Tens	Ones
3	1

Step 1
Add the ones.
2 + 9 = 11   19
Regroup the ones.
11 ones = 1 ten 1 one
Step 2
Add the tens.
10 + 10 + 10 = 30
So, 12 + 19 = 31.

11.
```
Tens   Ones
  1      6
+ 1      8
  3      4      16
```
Step 1
Add the ones.
6 + 8 = 14
Regroup the ones.   18
14 ones = 1 ten 4 ones
Step 2
Add the tens.
10 + 10 + 10 = 30
So, 16 + 18 = 34.

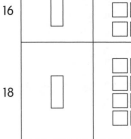

Tens	Ones
3	4

12. **Step 1** 7 + 3 = 10
    Regroup the ones.
    10 ones = 1 ten 0 ones
    Step 2 10 + 20 + 10 = 40
    So, 27 + 13 = 40.

```
Tens   Ones
  2      7
+ 1      3
  4      0
```

13. **Step 1** 7 + 5 = 12
    Regroup the ones.
    12 ones = 1 ten 2 ones
    Step 2 10 + 10 + 10 = 30
    So, 17 + 15 = 32.

```
Tens   Ones
  1      7
+ 1      5
  3      2
```

14.
```
Tens   Ones
  1      9
+ 1      3
  3      2
```

15.
```
Tens   Ones
  1      2
+ 2      8
  4      0
```

16.
```
  1   6
+ 1   5
  3   1
```

17.
```
  1   4
+ 1   8
  3   2
```

Worksheet 3

1. 19 − 7 = 12
    (10) (9)

2. 18 − 4 = 14
    (10) (8)

3. 11 − 5 = 6
    (1) (10)

4. 13 − 6 = 7
    (3) (10)

5. $\underline{10} - \underline{4} = \underline{6}$

6. $\underline{17} - \underline{9} = \underline{8}$

7. $\underline{14} - \underline{5} = \underline{9}$

8. 25, 24, 23, 22, 21
   $25 - 4 = \underline{21}$

9. 34, 33, 32
   $34 - 2 = \underline{32}$

10. 38, 37, 36, 35, 34, 33
    $38 - 5 = \underline{33}$

11.
```
Tens  Ones
 2     4
-      4
 2     0
```
24

Step 1
Subtract the ones.
$4 - 4 = \underline{0}$
Step 2
Subtract the tens.
$20 - 0 = \underline{20}$
So, $24 - 4 = \underline{20}$.

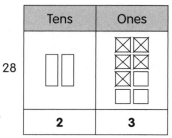

Tens	Ones
2	**0**

12.
```
Tens  Ones
 2     8
-      5
 2     3
```
28

Step 1
Subtract the ones.
$8 - 5 = \underline{3}$
Step 2
Subtract the tens.
$20 - 0 = \underline{20}$
So, $28 - 5 = \underline{23}$.

Tens	Ones
2	**3**

13.
```
Tens  Ones
 3     6
-      3
 3     3
```
36

Step 1
Subtract the ones.
$\underline{6} - \underline{3} = \underline{3}$
Step 2
Subtract the tens.
$\underline{30} - \underline{0} = \underline{30}$
So, $\underline{36} - \underline{3} = \underline{33}$.

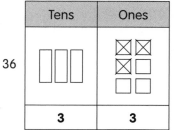

Tens	Ones
3	**3**

14. **Step 1** $9 - 8 = \underline{1}$
    Step 2 $20 - 0 = \underline{20}$
    So, $29 - 8 = \underline{21}$.

```
Tens  Ones
 2     9
-      8
 2     1
```

15. **Step 1** $7 - 4 = \underline{3}$
    Step 2 $30 - 0 = \underline{30}$
    So, $37 - 4 = \underline{33}$.

```
Tens  Ones
 3     7
-      4
 3     3
```

16.
```
Tens  Ones
 3     9
-      6
 3     3
```

17.
```
Tens  Ones
 2     7
-      3
 2     4
```

18.
```
 2     5
-      5
 2     0
```

19.
```
 3     6
-      4
 3     2
```

20.
```
Tens  Ones
 2     9
- 1    4
 1     5
```
29

Step 1
Subtract the ones.
$9 - 4 = \underline{5}$
Step 2
Subtract the tens.
$20 - 10 = \underline{10}$
So, $29 - 14 = \underline{15}$.

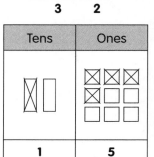

Tens	Ones
1	**5**

21.
```
Tens  Ones
 3     7
- 1    6
 2     1
```
37

Step 1
Subtract the ones.
$7 - 6 = \underline{1}$
Step 2
Subtract the tens.
$30 - 10 = \underline{20}$
So, $37 - 16 = \underline{21}$.

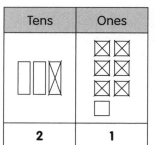

Tens	Ones
2	**1**

22.

Tens	Ones
3	2
− 2	0
1	**2**

32

Tens	Ones
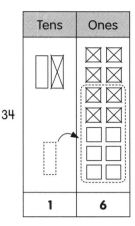	
1	**2**

Step 1

Subtract the ones.

$\underline{2} - \underline{0} = \underline{2}$

Step 2

Subtract the tens.

$\underline{30} - \underline{20} = \underline{10}$

So, 32 − 20 = $\underline{12}$.

23. Step 1 4 − 0 = $\underline{4}$

Step 2 20 − 10 = $\underline{10}$

So, 24 − 10 = $\underline{14}$.

Tens	Ones
2	4
− 1	0
1	**4**

24. Step 1 $\underline{6} - \underline{3} = \underline{3}$

Step 2 $\underline{30} - \underline{20} = \underline{10}$

So, 36 − 23 = $\underline{13}$.

Tens	Ones
3	6
− 2	3
1	**3**

25.

Tens	Ones
3	4
− 2	1
1	**3**

26.

Tens	Ones
2	8
− 1	6
1	**2**

27.

Tens	Ones
4	0
− 2	0
2	**0**

28.

Tens	Ones
3	5
− 1	2
2	**3**

Worksheet 4

1.

Tens	Ones		Tens	Ones
2	4	=	1	**14**

2.

Tens	Ones		Tens	Ones
3	3	=	2	**13**

3.

Tens	Ones		Tens	Ones
3	7	=	**2**	**17**

4.

Tens	Ones
²3̶	¹4
− 1	8
1	**6**

Step 1

Subtract the ones.
Regroup the tens
and ones in 34.

34 = 3 tens 4 ones

= 2 tens 14 ones

14 − 8 = $\underline{6}$

Step 2

Subtract the tens.

20 − 10 = $\underline{10}$

So, 34 − 18 = $\underline{16}$.

34

Tens	Ones
1	**6**

5.

Tens	Ones
¹2̶	³3
− 1	7
	6

Step 1

Subtract the ones.
Regroup the tens
and ones in 23.

23 = 2 tens 3 ones

= 1 ten 13 ones

13 − 7 = $\underline{6}$

Step 2

Subtract the tens.

10 − 10 = $\underline{0}$

So, 23 − 17 = $\underline{6}$.

23

Tens	Ones
	6

6.

Tens	Ones
²3̶	¹6
− 1	7
1	**9**

Step 1

Subtract the ones.
Regroup the tens and ones in 36.

3 tens 6 ones = 2 tens $\underline{16}$ ones

$\underline{16} - \underline{7} = \underline{9}$

Step 2

Subtract the tens.

$\underline{20} - \underline{10} = \underline{10}$

So, 36 − 17 = $\underline{19}$.

7.

Tens	Ones
¹2̸	6
−	9
1	**7**

26 → (20)(6) ➤ 26 → (10)(16)

8.

Tens	Ones
²3̸	¹4
−	7
2	**7**

34 → (30)(4) ➤ 34 → (20)(14)

9.

Tens	Ones
¹2̸	¹1
−	5
1	**6**

10.

Tens	Ones
¹2̸	¹5
−	8
1	**7**

11.

²3̸	¹0
−	4
2	**6**

12.

²3̸	¹3
−	6
2	**7**

13.

Tens	Ones
¹2̸	¹2
− 1	7
	5

22 → (20)(2) ➤ 22 → (10)(12)

14.

Tens	Ones
²3̸	¹1
− 1	3
1	**8**

31 → (30)(1) ➤ 31 → (20)(11)

15.

Tens	Ones
²3̸	¹5
− 2	9
	6

35 → (30)(5) ➤ 35 → (20)(15)

16.

¹2̸	¹4
− 1	5
	9

17.

¹2̸	¹7
− 1	9
	8

18.

²3̸	¹3
− 1	4
1	**9**

19.

³4̸	¹0
− 2	1
1	**9**

Worksheet 5

1. 8 + 9 + 3 = <u>20</u>

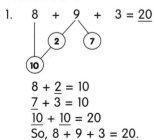

$8 + \underline{2} = 10$
$\underline{7} + 3 = 10$
$\underline{10} + \underline{10} = 20$
So, $8 + 9 + 3 = \underline{20}$.

2. 7 + 5 + 2 = <u>14</u>

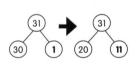

$7 + \underline{3} = 10$
$\underline{2} + 2 = 4$
$\underline{10} + \underline{4} = 14$
So, $\underline{7} + 5 + \underline{2} = \underline{14}$.

3. 6 + 8 + 4 = 18

$8 + \underline{2} = 10$
$6 + \underline{2} = 8$
$\underline{10} + \underline{8} = \underline{18}$
So, $\underline{6} + \underline{8} + \underline{4} = \underline{18}$.

4. 16   5. 21

Worksheet 6

1. 11 + 5 = 16
   Ryan used <u>16</u> shapes to make his picture.

2. 15 − 3 = 12
   Anna bakes <u>12</u> muffins.

3. 24 − 7 = 17
   Her brother read <u>17</u> books last month.

4. 27 + 9 = 36
   Alexis caught <u>36</u> spiders.

5. 21 + 14 = 35
   Susan buys <u>35</u> stamps.

6. 28 − 15 = 13
   Mr. Rogers had <u>13</u> caps left.

7. 19 + 11 = 30
   Karen makes <u>30</u> friendship bracelets.

8. 33 − 18 = 15
   Alan has <u>15</u> pencils.

9. 6 + 7 = 13
   13 + 4 = 17
   There are <u>17</u> toy cars in the big box.

10. 3 + 5 = 8
    8 + 7 = 15
    <u>15</u> children celebrate their birthdays in January and February.

Chapter 14

Worksheet 1

1. (10) → (1)(9)

2. (number bond) 10 → 3, 7

3. (number bond) 8 → 6, 2

4. (number bond) 9 → 4, 5

5. $4 + 8 = \underline{12}$
$8 + \underline{4} = \underline{12}$
$\underline{12} - \underline{4} = 8$
$\underline{12} - \underline{8} = 4$

6. $7 + 9 = \underline{10} + \underline{6}$
$= \underline{16}$

7. $8 + 5 = \underline{10} + \underline{3}$
$= \underline{13}$
(number bond) $8 +$ 5 → 2, 3

8. 6

9. 14

10. $4 + 5 = 4 + \underline{4} + \underline{1}$
$= \underline{8} + 1$
$= \underline{9}$

11. $8 + 7 = \underline{1} + \underline{7} + 7$
$= 1 + \underline{14}$
$= \underline{15}$

12. $\underline{1} + 8 = \underline{9}$
$10 + \underline{9} = \underline{19}$
So, $11 + 8 = \underline{19}$.
(number bond) 11 → 10, 1

13. $\underline{4} + 5 = \underline{9}$
$\underline{20} + 9 = \underline{29}$
So, $24 + 5 = \underline{29}$.
(number bond) 24 → 20, 4

14. $\underline{2} + 6 = \underline{8}$
$\underline{30} + 8 = \underline{38}$
So, $32 + 6 = \underline{38}$.
(number bond) 32 → 30, 2

15. 17

16. 18

17. 29

18. 28

19. 35

20. 38

21. $\underline{10} + 10 = \underline{20}$
$4 + \underline{20} = \underline{24}$
So, $14 + 10 = \underline{24}$.
(number bond) 14 → 10, 4

22. $\underline{20} + 10 = \underline{30}$
$\underline{7} + \underline{30} = \underline{37}$
So, $27 + 10 = \underline{37}$.
(number bond) 27 → 20, 7

23. $\underline{20} + 10 = \underline{30}$
$\underline{5} + \underline{30} = \underline{35}$
So, $20 + 15 = \underline{35}$.
(number bond) 15 → 10, 5

24. 29

25. 21

26. 38

27. 32

28. 37

29. 33

30. $5 + 6 = 5 + \underline{5} + \underline{1}$
$= \underline{10} + 1$
$= \underline{11}$

31. $3 + 4 = 3 + \underline{3} + \underline{1}$
$= \underline{6} + 1$
$= \underline{7}$

32. 17

33. 13

34. 27

35. 24

Worksheet 2

1. (number bond) 7 → 3, 4
4

2. (number bond) 13 → 5, 8
8

3. 3

4. 9

5. 4

6. 9

7. $\underline{5} - 2 = \underline{3}$
$20 + \underline{3} = \underline{23}$
So, $25 - 2 = \underline{23}$.
(number bond) 25 → 20, 5

8. $\underline{4} - 3 = \underline{1}$
$30 + \underline{1} = \underline{31}$
So, $34 - 3 = \underline{31}$.
(number bond) 34 → 30, 4

9. 21

10. 24

11. 30

12. 32

13. $20 - \underline{10} = \underline{10}$
$7 + \underline{10} = \underline{17}$
So, $27 - 10 = \underline{17}$.
(number bond) 27 → 20, 7

14. $30 - \underline{20} = \underline{10}$
$5 + \underline{10} = \underline{15}$
So, $35 - 20 = \underline{15}$.
(number bond) 35 → 30, 5

15. 19

16. 2

17. 14
18. 9
19. 8
20. 26

Chapter 15

Worksheet 1

1.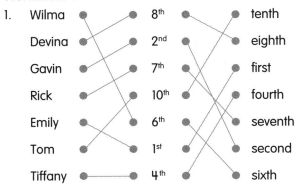

Wilma — 8th — tenth
Devina — 2nd — eighth
Gavin — 7th — first
Rick — 10th — fourth
Emily — 6th — seventh
Tom — 1st — second
Tiffany — 4th — sixth

2. 7
3. Sunday
4. Thursday
5. Monday
6. Thursday
7. 12
8. April
9. tenth
10. August
11. 28
12. 4
13. Wednesday
14–20.

2015

January						
Sunday	Monday	Tuesday	Wednesday	Thursday	Friday	Saturday
				1	2	3
④	5	6	⑦	8	⑨	10
11	12	⑬	14	15	16	17
18	19	20	2̶1̶	22	23	24
25	2̶6̶	27	28	2̶9̶	30	31

21. spring
22. summer
23. fall
24. winter
25. summer

26. fall
27. spring
28. winter

Worksheet 2

1. 11 o'clock
2. 2 o'clock
3. 8 o'clock
4. 5 o'clock
5. 2 o'clock
6. 8 o'clock
7. 11 o'clock
8. 3 o'clock
9. 7 o'clock
10. 1 o'clock
11.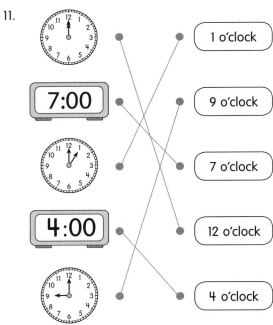

7:00 — 1 o'clock
— 9 o'clock
4:00 — 7 o'clock
— 12 o'clock
— 4 o'clock

12. 8 o'clock
13. 5 o'clock
14. 6:00   6 o'clock
15. 12:00   12 o'clock
16. 3 o'clock
17. 8 o'clock

18.  2:00

19. 4:00

Worksheet 3
1. half past 4
2. half past 7
3. half past 9
4. half past 12
5. half past 3
6. half past 7
7. half past 11
8. half past 9
9. half past 5
10. half past 2
11.

2:30 — half past 11

— half past 8

11:30 — half past 5

— half past 6

— half past 2

12. half past 4
13. half past 6
14. 8:30   half past 8
15. 12:30   half past 12

16. half past 11
17. half past 2
18. half past 4
19.  8:30
20. 5:30

Chapter 16

Worksheet 1
1. 5; 50
2. 6; 60
3. 7; 70
4. 8; 80
5. 9; 90
6. 10; 100
7. 10, ... 20, ... 30, ... 40, ... <u>50</u>, ... <u>60</u>, <u>61</u>, <u>62</u>, <u>63</u>
8. 10, ... 20, ... 30, ... 40, ... <u>50</u>, ... <u>60</u>, ... <u>70</u>, <u>71</u>, <u>72</u>, <u>73</u>, <u>74</u>, <u>75</u>, <u>76</u>
9. 10, ... 20, ... 30, ... 40, ... <u>50</u>, ... <u>60</u>, ... <u>70</u>, ... <u>80</u>, <u>81</u>, <u>82</u>, <u>83</u>, <u>84</u>, <u>85</u>
10. 10, ... 20, ... 30, ... 40, ... <u>50</u>, ... <u>60</u>, ... <u>70</u>, ... <u>80</u>, ... <u>90</u>, <u>91</u>, <u>92</u>
11. 103
12. 108
13. 115
14. 10, ... 20, ... 30, ... 40, ... <u>50</u>, ... <u>60</u>, ... <u>70</u>, ... <u>80</u>, ... <u>90</u>, ... <u>100</u>, <u>101</u>, <u>102</u>, <u>103</u>, <u>104</u>
15. 10, ... 20, ... 30, ... 40, ... <u>50</u>, ... <u>60</u>, ... <u>70</u>, ... <u>80</u>, ... <u>90</u>, ... <u>100</u>, ... <u>110</u>, <u>111</u>, <u>112</u>, <u>113</u>
16. 116   17. 109   18. 120
19. 112   20. 107   21. 113
22. one hundred three
23. one hundred five
24. one hundred eleven
25. one hundred nineteen
26. one hundred fourteen
27. one hundred eight

28. 60　　29. 83　　30. 1
31. 78　　32. 9　　33. 40
34. 30

Worksheet 2

1.
Tens	Ones
7	**9**

2.
Tens	Ones
6	**5**

3.
Tens	Ones
5	**3**

$53 = \underline{5}$ tens $\underline{3}$ ones
$53 = \underline{50} + \underline{3}$

4.
Tens	Ones
8	**7**

$\underline{87} = \underline{8}$ tens $\underline{7}$ ones
$\underline{87} = \underline{80} + \underline{7}$

5.
Tens	Ones
4	**9**

$\underline{49} = \underline{4}$ tens $\underline{9}$ ones
$\underline{49} = \underline{40} + \underline{9}$

6.
Tens	Ones
5	**4**

7.
Tens	Ones
9	**5**

8.
Tens	Ones
6	**9**

Worksheet 3

1. 65　　　　　　2. 62
3. 68　　　　　　4. 55
5. 56　　　　　　6. 70
7. 47　49　51　53　55　57
   45　46　48　50　52　54　56　58
8. 50　　　　　　9. 56
10. 56　　　　　11. 48
12. 54　　　　　13. 53
14. 46　　　　　15. 56

16. $\underline{7}$ tens is greater than $\underline{5}$ tens.
So, $\underline{70}$ is greater than $\underline{54}$.
$\underline{54}$ is less than $\underline{70}$.

17. $\underline{9}$ ones is greater than $\underline{7}$ ones.
So, $\underline{89}$ is greater than $\underline{87}$.
$\underline{87}$ is less than $\underline{89}$.

18. (81)　　　　19. (74)
20. (69)　　　　21. (48)
22. /53\　　　　23. /64\
24. /56\　　　　25. /90\
26. 62; 91　　　27. 43; 49
28. $\underline{70}$, $\underline{90}$, $\underline{100}$
    least　　　　greatest
29. $\underline{48}$, $\underline{46}$, $\underline{43}$
    greatest　　　　least
30. 60, 59, 58, $\underline{57}$, $\underline{56}$, 55, 54, $\underline{53}$
31. 47, 51, 55, 59, $\underline{63}$, $\underline{67}$
32. 46, 52, 58, $\underline{64}$, 70, $\underline{76}$, $\underline{82}$, 88
33. 83, $\underline{81}$, $\underline{79}$, 77, 75, 73
34. $\underline{76}$, $\underline{73}$, 70, 67, 64, 61
35. >　　36. =　　37. <
38. <　　39. >　　40. =
41. <　　42. >　　43. >

Chapter 17

Worksheet 1

1. $24 + 4 = \underline{28}$
   (20) (4)

2. $37 + 2 = \underline{39}$
   (30) (7)

3.
```
    2   5
+       2
    2   7
```

4.
```
    3   1
+       4
    3   5
```

5.
```
    1   4
+   1   2
    2   6
```

6.
```
    2   3
+   1   5
────────
    3   8
```

7. 66

8. 78

9. 98

10. 88

11.
```
   Tens  Ones
     5    4
+         3
────────────
     5    7
```
Step 1
Add the ones.
4 + 3 = <u>7</u>
Step 2
Add the tens.
50 + 0 = <u>50</u>
So, 54 + 3 = <u>57</u>.

12.
```
   Tens  Ones
     7    1
+         8
────────────
     7    9
```
Step 1
Add the ones.
1 + 8 = <u>9</u>
Step 2
Add the tens.
70 + 0 = <u>70</u>
So, 71 + 8 = <u>79</u>.

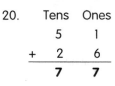

Tens	Ones
71	
8	
7	**9**

13.
```
   Tens  Ones
     4    2
+         6
────────────
     4    8
```
Step 1
Add the ones.
<u>2</u> + <u>6</u> = <u>8</u>
Step 2
Add the tens.
<u>40</u> + <u>0</u> = <u>40</u>
So, 42 + 6 = <u>48</u>.

Tens	Ones
42	
6	
4	**8**

14. **Step 1** 3 + 5 = <u>8</u>
Step 2 70 + 0 = <u>70</u>
So, 73 + 5 = <u>78</u>.

```
   Tens  Ones
     7    3
+         5
────────────
     7    8
```

15. **Step 1** <u>1</u> + <u>8</u> = <u>9</u>
Step 2 <u>80</u> + <u>0</u> = <u>80</u>
So, 81 + 8 = <u>89</u>.

```
   Tens  Ones
     8    1
+         8
────────────
     8    9
```

16.
```
   Tens  Ones
     9    1
+         5
────────────
     9    6
```

17.
```
   Tens  Ones
     8    3
+         4
────────────
     8    7
```

18.
```
     6    3
+         3
────────────
     6    6
```

19.
```
     7    7
+         2
────────────
     7    9
```

20.
```
   Tens  Ones
     5    1
+    2    6
────────────
     7    7
```
Step 1
Add the ones.
1 + 6 = <u>7</u>
Step 2
Add the tens.
50 + 20 = <u>70</u>
So, 51 + 26 = <u>77</u>.

21.
```
   Tens  Ones
     6    5
+    2    3
────────────
     8    8
```
Step 1
Add the ones.
5 + 3 = <u>8</u>
Step 2
Add the tens.
60 + 20 = <u>80</u>
So, 65 + 23 = <u>88</u>.

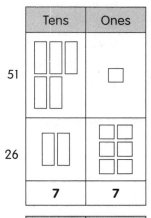

Tens	Ones
51	
26	
7	**7**

Tens	Ones
65	
23	
8	**8**

22.

Tens	Ones
6	3
+ 3	2
9	**5**

Step 1
Add the ones.
$\underline{3} + \underline{2} = \underline{5}$
Step 2
Add the tens.
$\underline{60} + \underline{30} = \underline{90}$
So, 63 + 32 = $\underline{95}$.

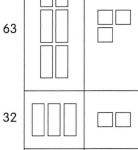

Tens	Ones
9	**5**

63
32

23. **Step 1** 3 + 5 = $\underline{8}$
Step 2 40 + 30 = $\underline{70}$
So, 43 + 35 = $\underline{78}$.

Tens	Ones
4	3
+ 3	5
7	**8**

24. **Step 1** $\underline{8} + \underline{1} = \underline{9}$
Step 2 $\underline{10} + \underline{40} = \underline{50}$
So, 18 + 41 = $\underline{59}$.

Tens	Ones
1	8
+ 4	1
5	**9**

25.

Tens	Ones
7	8
+ 1	0
8	**8**

26.

Tens	Ones
4	7
+ 1	2
5	**9**

27.

6	3
+ 3	6
9	**9**

28.

5	2
+ 2	4
7	**6**

Worksheet 2

1.

Tens	Ones		Tens	Ones
	48	=	4	**8**

2.

Tens	Ones		Tens	Ones
	36	=	**3**	6

3.

Tens	Ones		Tens	Ones
	62	=	6	**2**

4.

Tens	Ones		Tens	Ones
	99	=	**9**	**9**

5.

Tens	Ones
4	9
+	9
5	**8**

Step 1
Add the ones.
$9 + 9 = \underline{18}$
Regroup the ones.
$\underline{18}$ ones = 1 ten 8 ones
Step 2
Add the tens.
$10 + 40 + 0 = \underline{50}$
So, 49 + 9 = $\underline{58}$.

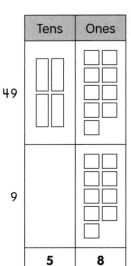

Tens	Ones
5	**8**

49
9

6.

Tens	Ones
5	8
+	5
6	**3**

Step 1
Add the ones.
$\underline{8} + \underline{5} = \underline{13}$
Regroup the ones.
$\underline{13}$ ones = $\underline{1}$ ten $\underline{3}$ ones
Step 2
Add the tens.
$\underline{10} + \underline{50} + \underline{0} = \underline{60}$
So, 58 + 5 = $\underline{63}$.

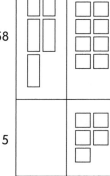

Tens	Ones
6	**3**

58
5

7.

Tens	Ones
6	7
+	5
7	**2**

Step 1
$7 + 5 = \underline{12}$
Regroup the ones.
$\underline{12}$ ones = 1 ten 2 ones
Step 2
$10 + 60 + 0 = \underline{70}$
So, 67 + 5 = $\underline{72}$.

8.

Tens	Ones
4	5
+	5
5	**0**

Step 1

$5 + 5 = \underline{10}$
Regroup the ones.
$\underline{10}$ ones = $\underline{1}$ ten $\underline{0}$ ones

Step 2

$\underline{10} + \underline{40} + \underline{0} = \underline{50}$
So, $45 + 5 = \underline{50}$.

9.

5	6
+	8
6	**4**

10.

8	7
+	3
9	**0**

11.

Tens	Ones
4	4
+ 1	9
6	**3**

Step 1

Add the ones.
$4 + 9 = \underline{13}$
Regroup the ones.
$\underline{13}$ ones = 1 ten 3 ones

Step 2

Add the tens.
$\underline{10} + \underline{40} + \underline{10} = \underline{60}$
So, $44 + 19 = \underline{63}$.

12.

Tens	Ones
5	8
+ 2	5
8	**3**

Step 1

Add the ones.
$\underline{8} + \underline{5} = \underline{13}$
Regroup the ones.
$\underline{13}$ ones = $\underline{1}$ ten $\underline{3}$ ones

Step 2

Add the tens.
$\underline{10} + \underline{50} + \underline{20} = \underline{80}$
So, $58 + 25 = \underline{83}$.

Tens	Ones
44	
19	
6	**3**

Tens	Ones
58	
25	
8	**3**

13.

Tens	Ones
5	8
+ 1	3
7	**1**

Step 1

$8 + 3 = \underline{11}$
Regroup the ones.
$\underline{11}$ ones = 1 ten 1 one

Step 2

$10 + 50 + 10 = \underline{70}$
So, $58 + 13 = \underline{71}$.

14.

Tens	Ones
2	7
+ 6	5
9	**2**

Step 1

$\underline{7} + \underline{5} = \underline{12}$
Regroup the ones.
$\underline{12}$ ones = $\underline{1}$ ten $\underline{2}$ ones

Step 2

$\underline{10} + \underline{20} + \underline{60} = \underline{90}$
So, $27 + 65 = \underline{92}$.

15.

Tens	Ones
7	2
+ 1	9
9	**1**

16.

Tens	Ones
6	2
+ 2	8
9	**0**

17.

3	9
+ 2	8
6	**7**

18.

2	4
+ 5	8
8	**2**

Worksheet 3

1. $2\underline{8} - 3 = \underline{25}$
   20   8

2. $35 - 2 = \underline{33}$
   30   5

3.
```
      2   5
  –       2
      2   3
```

4.
```
      3   9
  –       4
      3   5
```

5.
```
      2   2
  –   1   0
      1   2
```

6.
```
      3   8
  –   1   3
      2   5
```

7. 93

8. 72

9. 80

10. 61

11.
```
   Tens   Ones
     4      8
  –         6
     4      2
```

Step 1

Subtract the ones.
8 – 6 = 2

Step 2

Subtract the tens.
40 – 0 = 40
So, 48 – 6 = 42.

48
Tens	Ones
4	2

12.
```
   Tens   Ones
     4      4
  –         3
     4      1
```

Step 1

Subtract the ones.
4 – 3 = 1

Step 2

Subtract the tens.
40 – 0 = 40
So, 44 – 3 = 41.

44
Tens	Ones
4	1

13.
```
   Tens   Ones
     6      9
  –         2
     6      7
```

Step 1

Subtract the ones.
9 – 2 = 7

Step 2

Subtract the tens.
60 – 0 = 60
So, 69 – 2 = 67.

69
Tens	Ones
6	7

14. **Step 1** 6 – 5 = 1
Step 2 70 – 0 = 70
So, 76 – 5 = 71.

```
   Tens   Ones
     7      6
  –         5
     7      1
```

15. **Step 1** 7 – 4 = 3
Step 2 50 – 0 = 50
So, 57 – 4 = 53.

```
   Tens   Ones
     5      7
  –         4
     5      3
```

16.
```
   Tens   Ones
     5      5
  –         5
     5      0
```

17.
```
   Tens   Ones
     8      8
  –         6
     8      2
```

18.
```
     4      6
  –         3
     4      3
```

19.
```
     6      9
  –         8
     6      1
```

20.
```
   Tens   Ones
     5      9
  –   2      5
     3      4
```

Step 1

Subtract the ones.
9 – 5 = 4

Step 2

Subtract the tens.
50 – 20 = 30
So, 59 – 25 = 34.

59
Tens	Ones
3	4

21.

Tens	Ones
6	8
− 4	4
2	4

Step 1

Subtract the ones.
8 − 4 = <u>4</u>

Step 2

Subtract the tens.
60 − 40 = <u>20</u>
So, 68 − 44 = <u>24</u>.

Tens	Ones

68

Tens	Ones
2	**4**

22.

Tens	Ones
7	7
− 3	6
4	1

Step 1

Subtract the ones.
<u>7</u> − <u>6</u> = <u>1</u>

Step 2

Subtract the tens.
<u>70</u> − <u>30</u> = <u>40</u>
So, 77 − 36 = <u>41</u>.

Tens	Ones

77

Tens	Ones
4	**1**

23. **Step 1** 9 − 5 = <u>4</u>
    Step 2 40 − 30 = <u>10</u>
    So, 49 − 35 = <u>14</u>.

Tens	Ones
4	9
− 3	5
1	4

24. **Step 1** <u>8</u> − <u>3</u> = <u>5</u>
    Step 2 <u>40</u> − <u>10</u> = <u>30</u>
    So, 48 − 13 = <u>35</u>.

Tens	Ones
4	8
− 1	3
3	5

25.

Tens	Ones
6	4
− 2	1
4	3

26.

Tens	Ones
5	7
− 1	6
4	1

27.

	7	0
−	5	0
	2	0

28.

	8	4
−	3	2
	5	2

Worksheet 4

1.

Tens	Ones		Tens	Ones
3	4	=	2	**14**

2.

Tens	Ones		Tens	Ones
4	3	=	3	**13**

3.

Tens	Ones		Tens	Ones
5	7	=	**4**	17

4.

Tens	Ones
⁵6̸	¹4
−	8
5	6

Step 1

Subtract the ones.
Regroup the tens
and ones in 64.
64 = 6 tens 4 ones
   = 5 tens 14 ones
14 − 8 = <u>6</u>

Step 2

Subtract the tens.
50 − 0 = <u>50</u>
So, 64 − 8 = <u>56</u>.

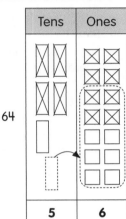

64

Tens	Ones
5	**6**

5. **Step 1**

Subtract the ones.
Regroup the tens and
ones in 82.
8 tens 2 ones = 7 tens <u>12</u> ones
<u>12</u> − <u>5</u> = <u>7</u>

Step 2

Subtract the tens.
<u>70</u> − <u>0</u> = <u>70</u>
So, 82 − 5 = <u>77</u>.

Tens	Ones
⁷8̸	¹2
−	5
7	7

6.
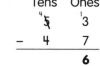

Tens	Ones
⁴5̶	¹3
− 4	7
	6

Step 1

Subtract the ones.
Regroup the tens
and ones in 53.
53 = 5 tens 3 ones
    = 4 tens 13 ones
13 − 7 = <u>6</u>

Step 2

Subtract the tens.
40 − 40 = <u>0</u>

So, 53 − 47 = <u>6</u>.

7.

Tens	Ones
⁶7̶	¹6
− 3	7
3	**9**

Step 1

Subtract the ones.
Regroup the tens and ones in 76.
7 tens 6 ones = 6 tens <u>16</u> ones
<u>16</u> − <u>7</u> = <u>9</u>

Step 2

Subtract the tens.
<u>60</u> − <u>30</u> = <u>30</u>

So, 76 − 37 = <u>39</u>.

8.

Tens	Ones
⁴5̶	¹2
−	6
4	**6**

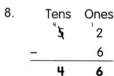

9.

Tens	Ones
⁵6̶	¹4
−	7
5	**7**

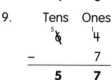

10.

Tens	Ones
⁸9̶	¹1
− 3	3
5	**8**

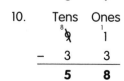

11.

Tens	Ones
³4̶	¹3
−	8
3	**5**

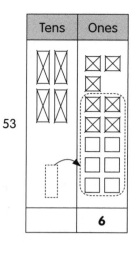

Tens	Ones
53	
	6

12.

Tens	Ones
⁷8̶	¹4
−	6
7	**8**

13.

Tens	Ones
⁶7̶	¹4
− 1	9
5	**5**

14.

Tens	Ones
⁵6̶	¹2
− 3	7
2	**5**

15.

⁵6̶	¹0
−	5
5	**5**

16.

⁸9̶	¹7
−	9
8	**8**

17.

⁴5̶	¹4
− 4	5
	9

18.

⁶7̶	¹3
− 4	4
2	**9**

Chapter 18

Worksheet 1

1. 6   2. 14   3. 12
4. 15   5. 16   6. 2
7. 12; 12   8. 21; 21   9. 24; 24
10.

9 + 9 + 9 + 9   5 groups of 5
4 groups of 2   6 fours
5 fives   2 + 2 + 2 + 2
8 + 8 + 8   4 nines
6 groups of 4   3 eights

11. <u>4</u> + <u>4</u> + <u>4</u> + <u>4</u> = <u>16</u>
       <u>4</u> fours = <u>16</u>
There are <u>16</u> tops in all.

12. $\underline{5} + \underline{5} + \underline{5} = \underline{15}$
$\underline{3}$ fives = $\underline{15}$
There are $\underline{15}$ strawberries in all.

13. $\underline{7} + \underline{7} + \underline{7} + \underline{7} = \underline{28}$
$\underline{4}$ sevens = $\underline{28}$
There are $\underline{28}$ candles in all.

14. There are $\underline{6}$ groups.
Each group has $\underline{5}$ hearts.
$5 + 5 + \underline{5} + \underline{5} + \underline{5} + \underline{5} = \underline{30}$
6 $\underline{fives}$ = $\underline{30}$
There are $\underline{30}$ hearts in all.

15. There are $\underline{4}$ groups.
Each group has $\underline{2}$ watermelons.
$\underline{4}$ $\underline{twos}$ = $\underline{8}$
There are $\underline{8}$ watermelons in all.

16. 50; 50

17. Each basket has $\underline{6}$ eggs.
7 $\underline{sixes}$ = $\underline{42}$
7 baskets have $\underline{42}$ eggs.

Worksheet 2

1. There are $\underline{8}$ keys in all.
There are $\underline{4}$ groups.
There are $\underline{2}$ keys in each group.

2. There are $\underline{24}$ oranges in all.
There are $\underline{4}$ bags.
There are $\underline{6}$ oranges in each bag.

3. There are $\underline{25}$ party hats in all.
There are $\underline{5}$ boxes.
There are $\underline{5}$ party hats in each box.

4. There are $\underline{21}$ cherries in all.
There are $\underline{3}$ cakes.
There are $\underline{7}$ cherries on each cake.

5. There are $\underline{12}$ frogs in all.
There are $\underline{4}$ lily pads.
There are $\underline{3}$ frogs on each lily pad.

6.
There are $\underline{4}$ smiley faces in each group.

7.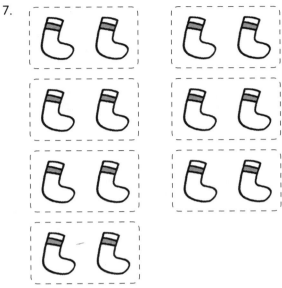
Each child gets $\underline{2}$ socks.

8.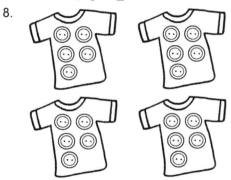
$\underline{5}$ buttons are sewed onto each T-shirt.

9.
There are $\underline{6}$ mugs in each group.

10.

There are <u>3</u> sea lions in each group.

11.

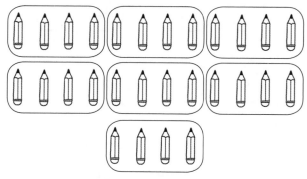

There are <u>4</u> pencils in each group.

12.

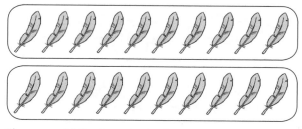

There are <u>10</u> feathers in each group.

Worksheet 3

1.

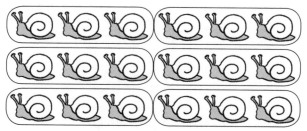

There are <u>6</u> groups of 3 snails.

2.

There are <u>5</u> groups of 5 cabbages.

3.

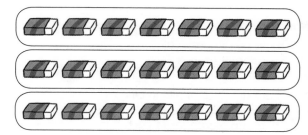

There are <u>3</u> groups of 7 erasers.

4.	4	5.	8
6.	9	7.	6

Chapter 19

Worksheet 1

1.	nickel	2.	penny
3.	dime	4.	nickel
5.	2¢	6.	5¢
7.	8¢	8.	penny; penny
9.	nickel; nickel	10.	10
11.	30	12.	12
13.	25	14.	20

15.

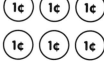

10

16. (5¢) (5¢)

2

17. (5¢) (1¢) (1¢) (1¢) (1¢) (1¢)

1; 5

18.

Coins	Items	Draw coins to show the same value in another way
	15¢	(10¢) (5¢)
	22¢	(5¢) (5¢) (5¢) (5¢) (1¢) (1¢)

6.

7.

8.

Coins	Value	Draw coins to show the value in another way
	52¢	Answers vary.

9.

	95¢	Answers vary.

Worksheet 2

1. 25
2. 5
3. 5
4. 2
5. (10¢) (10¢) (5¢)

6. (10¢) (5¢) (5¢) (5¢)

7. (5¢) (5¢) (5¢) (5¢) (5¢)

8. (10¢) (5¢) (5¢) (1¢) (1¢) (1¢) (1¢) (1¢)

Worksheet 3

1. 71
2. 29
3. 80
4. 87
5. Answers vary.

Worksheet 4

1. 100¢
2. 27¢; 39¢
3. $\underline{32¢} + \underline{20¢} = \underline{52¢}$
4. $\underline{56¢} + \underline{25¢} = \underline{81¢}$
5. $\underline{35¢} + \underline{20¢} = \underline{55¢}$ 6. $\underline{48¢} + \underline{41¢} = \underline{89¢}$
7. $\underline{8¢} + \underline{32¢} = \underline{40¢}$
   He spends $\underline{40¢}$.
8. $\underline{15¢} + \underline{15¢} + \underline{69¢} = \underline{99¢}$
   She spends $\underline{99¢}$.
9. 15¢; 25¢
10. $\underline{48¢} - \underline{36¢} = \underline{12¢}$
11. $\underline{59¢} - \underline{27¢} = \underline{32¢}$
12. $\underline{75¢} - \underline{12¢} = \underline{63¢}$
13. $\underline{75¢} - \underline{53¢} = \underline{22¢}$
14. $\underline{50¢} - \underline{30¢} = \underline{20¢}$
15. $\underline{27¢} - \underline{19¢} = \underline{8¢}$
16. $\underline{62¢} - \underline{42¢} = \underline{20¢}$
17. $\underline{76¢} - \underline{55¢} = \underline{21¢}$

18. Change = $\underline{38¢} - \underline{27¢}$
      = $\underline{11¢}$

19. Change = $\underline{70¢} - \underline{45¢}$
      = $\underline{25¢}$

20. Change = $\underline{65¢} - \underline{52¢}$
      = $\underline{13¢}$

21. Change = $\underline{100¢} - \underline{84¢}$
      = $\underline{16¢}$

22. 82¢ − 78¢ = 4¢
    Luke has $\underline{4¢}$ left.

23. 11¢ + 54¢ = 65¢
    She had $\underline{65¢}$ at first.

24. 80¢ − 50¢ = 30¢
    Sam pays $\underline{30¢}$ less than Brad.

25. 20¢ + 75¢ = 95¢
    Sucre has $\underline{95¢}$ in all.

26. 30¢ − 27¢ = 3¢
    Janice gets $\underline{3¢}$ in change.

Contents

Introducing

Math in Focus®

Enrichment

Written to complement *Math in Focus®: Singapore Math®* by *Marshall Cavendish* Grade 1, exercises in *Enrichment 1A* and *1B* are designed for advanced students seeking a challenge beyond the exercises and questions in the Student Books and Workbooks.

These exercises require children to draw on their fundamental mathematical understanding as well as recently acquired concepts and skills, combining problem-solving strategies with critical thinking skills.

Critical thinking skills enhanced by working on *Enrichment* exercises include classifying, comparing, sequencing, analyzing parts and whole, identifying patterns and relationships, induction (from specific to general), deduction (from general to specific), and spatial visualization.

One set of problems is provided for each chapter, to be assigned after the chapter has been completed. *Enrichment* exercises can be assigned while other students are working on the Chapter Review/Test, or while the class is working on subsequent chapters.